An Unexpected CHANCE

NEW YORK TIMES BESTSELLING AUTHOR
M MORELAND

INSTA-Spark

Dear Reader,

Thank you for selecting An Unexpected Chance to read. Be sure to sign up for my newsletter for up to date information on new releases, exclusive content and sales. You can find the form here: https://bit.ly/MMorelandNewsletter

Before you sign up, add melanie@melaniemoreland.com to your contacts to make sure the email comes right to your inbox! **Always fun - never spam!**

My books are available in paperback and audiobook! You can see all my books available and upcoming preorders at my website.

The Perfect Recipe For **LOVE**

xoxo,

Melanie

AN UNEXPECTED CHANCE by
M Moreland/Melanie Moreland
Copyright © 2023 Moreland Books Inc.
Copyright #1189142
Paperback 978-1-990803-30-7
All rights reserved

MORELAND
BOOKS INC.

Edited by Lisa Hollett of Silently Correcting Your Grammar
Proofreading by Sisters Get Lit.erary Author Services
Cover design by Karen Hulseman, Feed Your Dreams Designs
Cover Photography by Shutterstock
Cover content is for illustrative purposes only and any person
depicted on the cover is a model.

implied endorsement if any of these terms are used. The author acknowledges the trademarked status and trademark owners of various products referenced in this work of fiction, which have been used without permission. The publication/use of these trademarks is not authorized, associated with, or sponsored by the trademark owners.

Readers with concerns about content or subjects depicted can check out the content advisory on my website: https://melaniemoreland.com/extras/fan-suggestions/content-advisory/

CHAPTER ONE

SIMON

I poured a cup of coffee and walked outside, staring at the vista in front of me. I would never get tired of it. Coming from Ontario and the busy city we lived in, the openness of Nova Scotia was a delight to the eyes. This small town was the opposite of the noisy, bustling place we had left behind. From my porch, I could see the water, hear the waves as they crashed against the rocks. Watch the ever-changing colors in the depths. See storms as they approached. Mia and I loved to sit in the family room on the second floor and watch them roll in. We were fascinated by the way the clouds moved, the ocean joined with the skies to produce and echo the ferocity building in the air before the storm would strike. Mia would snuggle close, and I treasured those times with her.

My daughter—the nucleus of my world.

I ran a hand over my face, thinking of the letter

my lawyer had given me yesterday. It was from my ex-wife Kelsey, Mia's mother. She was like the proverbial bad penny and kept turning up. Subtlety and grace had never been her strong suits. Give me what I want was more up her alley.

I wasn't shocked when I read it, but still, anger and disappointment raged in me as I scanned the words.

There was no query about Mia. No second thoughts about wanting a relationship with her daughter. Instead, it was a 'woe is me, life isn't good, and you still owe me' letter. She wanted more money. If I was honest with myself, it was all she'd ever wanted from me. I had been blind to her when I met her. I fell for her beauty and the façade she showed to the world. Even after we were married and the screaming voices in my head told me it had been a mistake, I tried. I gave in to her tantrums, telling myself she was settling into our marriage. I ignored her jibes and constant cruel actions, allowing leeway for her age. The twelve-year difference between us became a sore spot for us over and again. When she told me she was pregnant, I was thrilled. I was certain being a mother would soften her, make her less shallow and more the person I had believed her to be.

It only got worse. It became obvious to me what a mistake I had made. She had married me for one reason and one reason only. My money. The breaking point came when I saw her true colors during the holiday season the first year Mia was born. Her brother showed up unexpectedly, and I was shocked not only to learn of his existence, but to witness the way he was treated. He didn't fit into the mold of the rest of her family. He sought neither money nor power, but simply to live his life and be happy. He was made so unwelcome, he left before I got a chance to know him. Shortly after, Kelsey and I separated. I paid a great deal of money to get rid of her, and she gave me the only thing I wanted from our marriage. My daughter. It had been a long, ugly fight, as well as costly, but a good trade being rid the poison Kelsey was in our lives.

Becoming a single father wasn't easy, but it was worth it. I concentrated on Mia and my work. My two main focuses. Our first Christmas alone, a small package arrived from Kelsey's brother Evan and his wife Holly with a gift in it for Mia. Every year after, a package would appear, and when Mia was old enough, she became curious about her uncle. She begged me to take her to visit, and once we arrived— and he got over the shock of our appearance—the relationship between them flourished. The added bonus was that my relationship with Evan, Holly, and their family did as well. What started as a holiday became permanent, and we moved here. Surrounded by the beautiful scenery and the warm people, I knew I'd made the right decision. Mia blossomed the past while and was excited to start school. Settling into the new house and getting her ready had been my main focus until the letter arrived yesterday.

I sat down on the swing Evan had made and helped me hang on the porch. I sipped my coffee, letting the tranquility around me settle my anger.

Kelsey was a piece of work, and while part of me wished I had figured that out before I married her, I wouldn't give up Mia for anything. But my ex wasn't getting another penny out of me. She could find someone else to bleed. My lawyer assured me she had zero chance of getting any rights back to Mia, so her subtle threats didn't sway me. And I owed her nothing. I'd given her a healthy settlement, bought her a new house, and paid off her debts to get rid of her. I had no feelings left for her aside from contempt. The truth was I had never truly loved her—I had loved the thought of her, of what we could be. When I saw the real person I married, I was horrified and had zero guilt about walking away. Mia and I were both better off without her.

Moving here to Cliff's Edge had been exactly what we needed. A fresh start. Mia was thriving, loving the dynamics of a small town, the family we had found, and the new house. I loved the peacefulness and the chance to watch her grow surrounded by love.

The front door opened, and she rushed out, her dark hair a mass of tangles. Her feet were shoved into slippers, and her pajamas were covered in unicorns. Her face broke into a wide smile.

"Hi, Daddy!"

Laughing, I braced myself as she launched into

my arms, the swing moving wildly. I pressed a kiss to her head.

"Hey, Sweet Pea. How'd you sleep?"

"So good. I love it here."

I kissed her again, enjoying her weight on my lap. "Me too."

"Are we going shopping?"

I tucked a lock of hair behind her ear. "You are going shopping with Auntie Holly and your cousins. I'm working."

She grinned, not at all bothered. She loved Holly.

"You don't like shopping, do you, Daddy?"

"Only in small doses. Holly can help you with clothes and supplies better than I can."

"What about groceries?"

"We only need a few things. I have to pick up a package at UPS, so I'll grab what we need while I'm in town. Holly is taking you into Halifax so there's a better selection." I glanced at my watch. "You have about an hour until she gets here."

"Will you do my hair?"

Of all the things I'd had to learn about being a single dad, that had been the most challenging. Hair. All I did with mine was wash it and let it dry. Let the barber trim it. Mia's long, thick locks were a challenge, but she refused to let me have it cut. So, I studied YouTube videos, asked the women at Mia's day care, and experimented over and over until I was proficient. I could French braid, twist, and upsweep with the best of them. Mia often did her own hair now, but I still liked it when she asked me.

"How do you want it?"

"Two braids."

"Sure. Go have breakfast and get dressed, and I'll do it."

She kissed my cheek and scampered away. "Love you, Daddy!" she called as she headed inside.

I smiled at her words, my heart warm. I drained my cup and stood. I would instruct my lawyer to write Kelsey a refusal and tell him to include a paragraph about no further contact. Hopefully she would get the message and move on. I was sure there was someone out there as detached as she was who she could sink her claws into. I was done.

Then I headed inside.

I had braids to weave.

CHAPTER TWO

SIMON

I looked at the cart in front of me with a wry smile. So much for only needing a few things. I may have aced the hair thing over the years, but my meal planning and grocery shopping hadn't improved that much. At least Mia had grown beyond chicken nuggets and fries. I swore that was all she ate for about three years. I kept our meals pretty simple. Grilled meat, salad, and whatever vegetables I could get into her was our usual. Luckily, she liked salad. That, I could do. Mac and cheese was a staple too. Thank God for Holly. We went to their house a lot, and Mia ate well there. Holly often sent home leftovers, which was a godsend. And she was an awesome cook.

I looked around the cookie aisle, dismissing most of it. Mia and I both had a huge sweet tooth, but once we'd tasted Holly's baking, nothing compared. Chips Ahoy! now tasted like cardboard. We did still like the maple cookies, so I added a package. I grabbed the handle of the cart, waiting as the woman beside me perused the shelves. There was something familiar about her, and I studied her, my pulse picking up as I recognized Amy McNeil. She was a friend of Holly's and had been at the last two barbecues they'd invited us to. She taught kindergarten at the school Mia would be attending, and we had chatted about the school and her classes. I found her intelligent and kind, with her gentle, raspy voice and warm personality. She was average height with rich blonde hair that hung down her back in wild curls and light blue eyes. She had a bohemian look with her layered skirt, scarf, and frilly blouse. Feminine and alluring. Pretty. She had a row of gold freckles across the bridge of her nose, if I remembered correctly. It gave her a mischievous look.

I cleared my throat, and she turned her head, her lovely eyes widening when she saw me.

"Simon Fletcher," she said, smiling.

My name coming from her mouth with the low rasp in her voice did something to my chest.

"Amy McNeil," I replied. "Shopping for cookies? I took you for a home baker."

She rolled her eyes. "Have you seen kindergartners inhale cookies? I always do cookies on the first day, but I get simple ones." She tapped her lip. "I was looking at these low-sugar ones."

I grimaced. "Why bother?"

She chuckled, spying the maple creams in my

basket. "Oh, those! Yes!" She clapped her hands. "Nut-free and kids love them. I can get myself some at the same time." Then she grimaced. "I'm blocking you in, aren't I?"

"Not a problem. Block me in anytime," I quipped, trying not to grin when color peaked on her cheeks.

She sidled past me, reaching for the maple cookies. She took four packages, then frowned and added two more. Meeting my amused glance, she shrugged. "They're on sale. Might as well stock up."

"Good point." I reached past her and grabbed two more packages. "They go great with Grape Nut ice cream."

"Oh my God. I love that. It's my favorite. So many people turn up their nose at it."

"It's Mia's favorite too."

She laid her hand on my arm. I glanced down at it, her fingers long and delicate. She had on three silver rings—all Celtic symbols—the thick metal glinting in the light. "How is Mia?"

"Great. Really great. She's shopping with Holly and the girls for school."

"Leaving you on your own to grocery shop?"

"It's best that way. I'm bad enough. Add Mia to the mix, I'm lucky to make it out with one cart. I can't seem to say no to her."

She smiled. "I like that."

"We're not good planners. It's whatever we decide we want and I've bought."

"You should do some freeze-ahead meals. I do them."

"What are those?"

"Oh, ah—"

I held up my hand. "Before you educate me, Amy, can I ask you something?"

"Sure?"

"Have you had lunch?"

"No."

"Can I interest you? In having lunch with me?"

She blinked. "Like, now?"

"Well, after we pay. Shoplifting is still a crime, I think."

She laughed, studied me for a moment, then nodded. "I would love to have lunch with you, Simon."

"Awesome. Let's finish up, and I'll follow you to wherever you want to go. I'm still learning the good places."

"I love The Cove. Lots of fresh seafood if you like that."

"Perfect." That was something I loved about this part of the country—the fresh fish and seafood you could get. I enjoyed it tremendously, and Mia was slowly learning her favorites.

Amy leaned closer, her scent swirling around me. Light, floral, with a citrus twist, it was pretty and unexpected. Just like her.

"Avoid JM's Tavern. It's, ah, not so nice. At all."

"Got it. Good thing I ran into you, then. I might have gone there."

She shuddered. "It would be the only time. Trust me."

I laughed. "Okay. How much more do you have to do?"

"I'm almost done. In fact, if you don't mind, I'll stop by my place and drop off the cold stuff." She paused. "You can borrow a shelf in the fridge if you want. Pick it up once we eat."

"Again, perfect." I swept my arm out. "Let's go."

———

I followed her to her apartment complex and grabbed the bag I needed to put in her refrigerator. I stopped at her car, taking a couple of her bags. "Leave your car here and come with me. I'll bring you back and get my groceries."

When she hesitated, I grinned. "Or take your car if you want an escape. I might chew with my mouth open or bore you to tears."

She laughed, shutting the lid of her trunk. "I highly doubt either. You chewed very nicely at the barbecue. You even managed not to get rib sauce all over your face, unlike me."

"And the boring part?" I asked, keeping my tone teasing even as echoes of Kelsey's mocking voice filled my head. *Such a bore, Simon. You are always such a bore.*

Amy shook her head, smiling at me over her

11

shoulder as she stopped by the door. "You could never bore me, Simon. I find you fascinating."

I smiled as I followed her up the steps.

In her apartment, I looked around, curious. It was her. Light, airy, with a fun, beachy feel. Blues, greens, and creams. Simple furniture. Driftwood. Seashells. Pictures of the ocean and some of our small town and the surrounding areas. I walked around, peering at them. When she came into the room, I tapped the one I was studying. "Great photos."

"Thanks. I took them."

"Wow—they're terrific."

She blushed prettily, making me want to touch her cheek to see if it was warm, but I refrained.

"I love your place," I commented.

She smiled, running a hand over her hair. "It's comfortable. I'm saving for a house, but it will be a while. I want one by the water."

"You like the beach," I said, indicating the shells and driftwood.

"I love the beach and the water. I sit and sketch or walk for miles. I love collecting stones or shells and making things with them."

"Mia would love that. She's starting to get into doing things with her hands. She draws really well."

"Maybe we can do it together one day," she offered, looking nervous.

I grinned. "Maybe." Without thinking, I held out my hand. "Lunch?"

She slipped her palm against mine with a smile. I

wrapped my fingers around hers, liking how it felt in mine.

"Sounds good," she replied.

The restaurant was fairly deserted. It was large, light, and open, overlooking the water. We got a table by the window, and Amy chatted to the server, obviously a regular. We ordered drinks, and I looked over the menu.

"What do you recommend?"

"The lobster and shrimp roll is spectacular. The grilled halibut is great too."

I shut my menu. "The roll for me."

She grinned. "Me too."

We ordered, and I lifted my wineglass, clinking it with hers. I sipped the cold white wine in appreciation and looked at the expanse of water through the window, feeling a smile tug on my mouth.

"What?" she asked, tilting her head to the side, studying me.

I shrugged, leaning my elbows on the table. "If someone had told me a few months ago that I would be living in Nova Scotia by the water, drinking wine at two o'clock on a weekday, sitting across from a beautiful lady, instead of my usual work from sunup to sundown, I would have laughed." I sat back, opening my hands. "Yet, here I am."

She smiled. "Change is good."

"It is."

She picked up her wine, studying her glass. "You think I'm beautiful?"

"Incredibly so. I thought it the moment I saw you at Evan's place. Even more so the last time."

"I thought you were incredibly sexy," she admitted.

I felt a glow of satisfaction. "Did you?" I murmured.

She lifted her eyes to mine, the blue almost silver in the sunlight. "You were laughing with Evan, and you looked so…virile and alive."

The glow became a fire.

"I think I was starting to fall in love with this place. Cliff's Edge is such an amazing little town. The people, the scenery, all of it. I hadn't expected to feel the way I did about it, but it felt as if I had found something I was looking for, if that makes sense."

She nodded. "I grew up in Halifax, but we often came out to Cliff's Edge, and I loved the vibe. I was working in Halifax when I saw the post for the position here. I applied and was thrilled to get the job."

"How long have you been here?"

"Five years." She sipped her wine. "Holly told me you brought Mia here to meet Evan."

I sat back, surprisingly relaxed, considering the subject. "I did. She wanted to meet her uncle. I never expected to find what we did. A family that opened their arms to us. A new life. But I've never seen Mia so happy or settled. I haven't felt this positive in years."

"Then it was meant to be."

Our lunch arrived, and I smiled. "I think it was."

The sandwiches were spectacular—stuffed with lobster and shrimp in a light dressing. The fries and salad that came with them added to the satisfaction, and we both enjoyed the meal thoroughly. There was no pretense with her. She picked up her sandwich, licking her thumb when some mayo dripped on it. She ate with gusto, not hiding the fact that she liked what she ate. It was refreshing. She was droll and smart.

As she chewed and swallowed, she lifted her eyebrows in question.

"You're settling in okay at the new house?"

"We love it. Mia is looking forward to school starting."

"Yes, she told me that at the last barbecue. She is very cute."

"I think so." I winked. "I thought you were pretty damn cute too."

"But you didn't make any moves."

"I wasn't ready," I admitted.

"But you are now?"

I studied her. "I think so. I would like to try anyway."

"I see."

"As long as you're on board with that."

Her cheeks colored.

"Yes. Yes, I am."

I grinned. "Excellent."

We kept the conversation light, exchanging tidbits about each other.

"Favorite movie?" I asked.

"Oh. Tied. *The Greatest Showman* and *The Last of the Mohicans*."

"Hmm. Never seen either."

"We'll have to rectify that."

"I'm not much into musicals. People don't really walk around bursting into song, you know," I teased.

She paused before taking a bite. "You haven't lived here long enough to know that." Then she winked and took a huge bite of her sandwich, a smear of mayo on the corner of her lips. I had to fight the urge to lean forward and remove it with my finger, then lick it off since it had been close to her full lips.

"Your favorite movies?" she asked.

"Oh, probably 007 or the Bourne series. I love Marvel movies too." I flashed a grin at her. "But usually, some Disney shit is blaring on the TV."

She laughed. "I bet you love it."

"Rapunzel is pretty badass. And I love Dory."

She snorted, covering her mouth with her hand. It

made me laugh, which made her laugh and snort again. It was endearing and I liked it.

"Maybe you'd like to come over and watch a movie with us," I suggested hopefully.

She paused. "I don't date parents of my kids. In fact, I rarely date."

"Mia isn't one of your students, and frankly, Ms. McNeil, we're already on a date. So, too late."

"I thought this was lunch."

"We had wine. It's a date."

"Well then, I suppose a movie is acceptable. I can teach you some cooking tips at the same time."

I pushed away my empty plate. "Awesome."

CHAPTER THREE

SIMON

Over coffee, the subject came up. Amy stirred cream into her cup, quiet until the server placed the piece of cheesecake between us and left.

"So, Mia's mother?" she asked quietly.

I sighed and sliced off a bite of cheesecake, chewing the dense richness slowly. I understood her question. She wasn't going to get involved with someone who might still have an ex and feelings.

"We split when Mia was a baby. Kelsey has not seen her once since then. Mia has no memory of her."

She gaped at me. "She hasn't seen her since she was a baby?"

I shook my head. "My ex wasn't the person I thought she was when I married her. She admitted to me she got pregnant to keep me, but we weren't compatible at all. She had zero maternal instincts and wanted nothing to do with Mia. She was, *is,* cold, cruel, and I'm grateful for the fact that she lives her own life. I don't want my daughter subjected to that sort of influence."

She reached across the table and covered my hand with hers. "I'm sorry."

I flipped my hand over, closing my fingers around hers. "It's fine. I built my life around Mia. I love her. I love being her dad. I regret my marriage but not my daughter."

"Does Mia ask about her?"

"She did once. I showed her a picture of her mother. She looked at it as if she were looking at a magazine ad. All she said was that she thought she looked more like me. She was far more interested in her uncle."

"Makes sense. The yearly gifts and all."

I had told her the whole story about Evan.

"Mia comes first with me. Always," I told her.

"As she should. I wish all parents were like you. I've seen a lot of people more like her mother than I can say."

She took a bite of cheesecake. "So, you have no contact with your ex?"

I barked a laugh. "When she wants something. She spends money like water. She sets up businesses and drains them, then decides I should help her with the next one. I'm sure her other ex-husbands get the same demands."

She lifted her eyebrows. "Others, as in, more than one?"

"Two others, I think. Plus, a never-ending turnaround of men. I gave up worrying about it a long time ago. Every so often, I get a letter via my lawyer, demanding money or wanting an investment. The first one, I panicked, thinking she'd come after Mia, and I sent her some money against Halton's advice. He was right—she kept coming back. The last one, she added a subtle threat about seeing Mia. But I've gotten wise, and maybe a little colder, and I shut that down fast. I had my lawyer start a cease and desist action. She gets nowhere near Mia or me. Or another damn cent. I paid her very well to walk away." I snorted. "Not that she needed much encouragement. All she wanted was the money. All I wanted was Mia and my freedom. It was an easy trade-off, although she made it as difficult as possible."

She squeezed my hand, and I realized I had been holding hers this whole time.

"It's been hard on you."

"I have Mia."

"You're a good man, Simon."

The conversation had gotten too serious. Too heavy. Needing to go back to the light, I winked at her. "Not such a good man that I'll let you have more than your share of that cheesecake, Amy." To make my point, I slid my hand away and pulled the plate closer, taking a large bite.

She laughed and picked up her coffee cup. She smiled indulgently. "Have at it. I have maple cookies at home."

I had to laugh. She was brilliant.

Back at her place, I got my bag of groceries and stood at her door, unsure what to say. I found I didn't want to leave her, yet I knew I had to go get Mia. Still, I lingered.

Amy was addictive. The rest of the lunch had been filled with sharing information. Grins and mutual laughter. She was witty and fun. Smart and clever. And kind. So kind. I liked how she treated people, spoke to them. She was honest, genuine. Real.

I drew in a deep breath. "I'd like to do the movie night, but I would also like to take you out first. Officially—on a date. I know you said you don't date much…" I laughed dryly. "I haven't been on a real date since before Mia was born so I'm pretty rusty, but I would like to take you out."

"I thought lunch went well as far as undates-dates go," she said with a smile.

"I think any time spent with you would be good," I admitted.

"So, you want to go out and test the waters— before having me spend time with Mia?" she asked.

"Yes," I replied honestly. "Mia—"

She cut me off. "I understand." She studied me

for a moment, coming to a decision. "I would like to go out with you, Simon. So, yes. I accept your offer."

"Friday?" I asked. "I'll figure out a nice place. Dinner, maybe a movie." I paused. "Do people do that for dates anymore?"

"It sounds good to me." Then her eyes widened. "There is a bar in Evansham—two towns over—they have music on Friday nights. Some local bands that are really good if you prefer. Some nice restaurants there too."

"Excellent. Any I should avoid?"

She shook her head. "Not that I've heard."

We exchanged cell numbers and agreed to seven o'clock on Friday. I bent to kiss her cheek, just as her head turned. Our mouths brushed, and we both froze. Then she moved, pressing her lips to mine, and I wrapped my arm around her waist, tugging her close, our mouths melded together.

Blistering heat bubbled under my skin at the feel and taste of her. She whimpered as my tongue slid along hers, and she slipped her arms around my neck. I explored her, the heat, the feel of her. How the taste of her coffee and the sweetness of the cheesecake we shared lingered in her mouth. How soft her lips were underneath mine. The thick, silky strands of her hair brushed my hand, and I wrapped my fist around them, enjoying the feel of them on my skin. Imagined how they would feel brushing against my thighs as she rode me with her head tilted back. I kissed her deeper, swimming in the sensations she brought forth. Want and desire. Need and longing. The urge for more. The passion that had lain dormant for so long exploded. I couldn't get close enough to her. Kiss her hard enough to satisfy my desire. Every second felt like an eternity, yet it wasn't enough. My body was on fire, my cock hard and aching. I wanted to pick her up and find her bed. Throw her onto the mattress and follow her down. Strip off the fabric separating us and bury myself inside her. Take her until she screamed my name in release.

I pulled back with a gasp before I did exactly that. She opened her eyes, the blue darker, her mouth swollen, her breathing coming fast. I traced her mouth with my finger. I had so much I wanted to say, but I couldn't.

"Thank you for lunch," she whispered.

"If that was thanks for lunch, I can't wait until dinner," I quipped.

She bit the end of my finger, and I laughed, my breath stuttering as she swiped her tongue over the end.

"Little vixen," I murmured, bending and kissing her again. Then I straightened and picked up the bag of groceries at my feet.

She watched me, her gaze all at once anxious and tender. I pressed one more kiss to her mouth. "Friday," I said. "I'll call before if that's okay."

"I look forward to it."

I walked away before I did something foolish, like call Holly and ask her to keep Mia, then follow through with my thoughts of carrying Amy down the hall.

I had to take this slow.

But I stopped before I turned the corner and looked back. Amy was watching me, a small smile on her face. She had her fingers pressed against her mouth as if keeping the feel of my lips there.

I winked as I went around the corner. I liked knowing she was watching me.

Suddenly, I could hardly wait until Friday.

AMY

Simon left, and I shut the door, leaning against the hard wood.

What the hell just happened?

Running into him at the grocery store wasn't surprising. It was a small town with only one larger place to shop. I ran into a lot of people there.

But they weren't Simon.

I had met Holly the first week I was in Cliff's Edge. Our carts literally ran into each other's in the store, and we got to talking. We became fast friends. After meeting Evan, I became close with the whole family, and I was always invited to their barbecues and family dinners. She had told me about the ex-brother-in-law showing up, and I was intrigued but only because his story was different. Few men would choose to be a single dad. At least, the ones I knew.

When we were introduced at Evan's barbecue, Simon had taken my breath away. Well over six feet, he had broad shoulders, and he carried himself well. His dark brown hair was short, his hazel eyes set under heavy brows, and he had a great smile. He was charming and funny, polite, and intelligent. I felt his interest, as well as the fact that he held himself back.

If you looked deep enough, his eyes held some lingering sadness. Holly had told me he was divorced and his ex-wife was cold and unfeeling. Holly didn't say much else except the ex had nothing to do with her brother, Evan, or her daughter. I assumed she'd done a number on Simon, which was why he held himself in check. Watching him with Mia made my heart melt. He obviously adored his daughter, and he had no problem displaying his affection. He was an excellent father—attentive and giving. Teasing and loving, yet firm with his denials when needed. I enjoyed watching the two of them together. Mia was a delight and seemed to relish spending time with her uncle, following him around a great deal. She was well-behaved and smart, an old soul in a little girl's body.

I had enjoyed talking to Simon. Our eyes met several times during the barbecue and we chatted more than once, but that was it. He was cordial and polite. I had left feeling oddly disappointed. When Holly told me he had decided to move here, I was secretly thrilled. When he'd shown up at the last barbecue, my interest piqued again, and I was happy to see him. Once again, we talked, but he didn't take it any further. I assumed his past made him wary, and I hoped we'd meet again.

The grocery store was the last place I'd thought I would meet him.

His teasing at the store made me smile. Seeing him caused a swell of happiness I couldn't totally explain. Knowing he was as invested in getting to know me as I was in him made me smile. I hadn't imagined the interest in his eyes. When he asked me to lunch, it was hard not to squeal, but I kept my cool.

He was everything I thought he would be. Charming, funny, sweet. Hearing what he had to say about his ex-wife made me sad. I couldn't imagine not falling in love with the sexy, confident man across from me. Only wanting him for his money. Walking away from my child. I couldn't fathom it. His voice was different as he spoke about her. Cold. Removed. Almost loathing.

But when he spoke of Mia, of their life together, he changed. Became the man filled with life I had seen. His eyes were tender, his voice loving as he talked about her.

"She's intelligent beyond her years, Amy. I mean, all parents think so, but she is. She was so bored in grade one, they moved her into grade two. When they assessed her here, they wanted to put her in grade four, but I asked to let her stay in three. I don't want her ostracized because of being younger or made fun of.

We do a lot of learning stuff together so she doesn't get bored. Maybe when she is a bit older, I'll let them push her ahead. But right now, I want her to be a kid, you know?" He smiled ruefully. "She's already growing too fast."

I thought he was smart with his decision, and I told him so. He seemed pleased.

When he accidentally kissed me in my apartment, I couldn't resist kissing him back. I wasn't prepared for his reaction or the depth and passion of his actions. I had never been kissed like that in my life. Carnal, deep, and commanding. The feel of his hard torso pressed against me, the evidence of his desire growing and swelling. His taste and his scent. The low groans of approval in his throat as he tugged me closer. I wanted to run my hands under his shirt. Feel his skin, have him kiss me even deeper, touch me, and let him know how wet he made me with just his kiss.

He was right to stop, but I knew we both teetered on the edge of not caring and giving in. His request for a date was pleasing, and I was looking forward to Friday night. To dinner with him. More of his laughter and teasing. More of his touches.

And, I hoped, more of his kisses.

CHAPTER FOUR

SIMON

Walking into Evan and Holly's house was like walking into a real home. You could sense the love that saturated the air. Pictures of them and their family were everywhere. Mementos of their travels. Little shoes and jackets hung up on pegs by the door. A wedding picture of them smiling widely at each other showed their happiness.

Dinner was cooking, the aroma mouthwatering. Evan was laughing and talking to one or more of the kids. I heard the sound of my daughter's amusement and knew she was wherever Uncle E was. They were very close.

I followed the sounds to the kitchen, chuckling at the sight that met my eyes. Holly and the girls were making cookies, the dough in misshapen balls on cookie sheets. The girls were wearing aprons but were still covered in flour and sugar. Evan was sitting at the table, encouraging the baking, teasing and egging them on.

I leaned on the doorframe, waiting until someone noticed me. Mia was the first, her little face brightening as she saw me.

"Daddy!" she exclaimed, launching off the chair. I bent, holding out my arms, not caring about the flour and sugar, but thrilled at the sweetness that was all her. She covered my face with kisses and told me about her shopping trip.

"I got the best shoes, Daddy! They sparkle!"

Her joy could not be contained.

"My new favorite shirt has a unicorn on it." Her eyes widened. "We found pink jeans! And hair ties to match!"

I laughed at her enthusiasm. "So you had a good day with Auntie Holly, Angela, and Hannah?"

"The best!"

I set her down on her feet. "Good."

"Did you do the grocery shopping?"

I tapped her nose. "Yes. And I got us maple cookies. But compared to what's going on here, they are a poor substitute."

Holly laughed and came over, pressing a kiss to my cheek. "We had a great day, and the girls wanted to bake. Chocolate chip cookies seemed in order."

"And I encouraged it," Evan said from across the room, bouncing Brandon on his knee. I crossed the room and sat at the table, snagging a fresh cookie and sitting back, enjoying watching the girls.

Holly glanced my way. "You're staying for dinner?" she asked, but it sounded more like a command.

"Well, I went grocery shopping, so we have food. But since it won't taste anywhere near as good as yours, the answer is yes."

"Great. You can look at all the stuff we bought."

"Can't wait."

After dinner, the kids ran outside, and we followed, settling in chairs as we watched them play.

"I'm so glad you're here," Holly mused. "The girls get along so well."

"They do," I agreed, sipping my coffee and having another fresh-made cookie.

"So, ah, do you have plans Friday night?" I asked casually.

"No," Evan replied, laying his arm across the back of the swing he and Holly shared. "Why?"

"Any chance you could look after Mia? Maybe let her spend the night?"

Holly grinned. "Anytime. She is always welcome."

Evan narrowed his eyes. "Where will you be? Some late work thing?"

I chuckled. "No. I have a date."

Holly leaned forward. "With Amy?"

"Yes. We bumped into each other at the store and ended up having a quick lunch. I asked her out."

Holly grinned, looking delighted. "Sure, we'll keep Mia. Right, Evan?"

"Of course."

Angela called for her mom, and Holly stood. "Don't be gossiping without me."

"We don't gossip, woman," Evan said.

"Whatever," she muttered and hurried away to help Angela.

He turned to me. "Amy, eh?"

I leaned back, sipping my coffee. "Yes, Amy."

"Holly noticed you talking to her at the last two barbecues. They're great friends. Well, we both are, I suppose, but they're pretty tight." He leaned close, resting his arms on his thighs. "Amy's really lovely. Kind and thoughtful. Sweet." He grinned. "A bit of a free spirit."

I chuckled. "She calls herself unconventional. I like it. She's a breath of fresh air. So calm and natural."

"Total opposite to Kelsey."

I nodded. We both muttered "Thank God" at the same time and laughed.

"I've had enough drama from your sister to last a lifetime. Amy seems far more...*normal*, I'll say."

"She know about Kelsey?"

"Enough for now. It's too soon. I haven't taken her to dinner yet—I'm not dumping all that shit on her."

Evan didn't say anything for a moment, then he spoke. "I'm sorry for what my sister did to you and Mia, Simon. You're a great guy, and you didn't deserve to go through that. But I'm not sorry it brought you into our lives. You've become part of the family. Holly adores you and Mia. I feel as if I got a brother as well as a friend. So, even though you went through hell, I'm glad you're here."

I studied him. "I wouldn't give up one moment of the shit I went through if it meant it brought me to this place and moment. Mia is worth everything I had to endure. She is my life. Getting the bonus of you and Holly and the kids? I consider myself a lucky man, Evan. A very lucky man."

We shared a nod. A silent assurance we understood each other.

Then he winked. "Okay, let's get you dating again. Where are you taking her?"

———

Friday afternoon, I shut down my laptop, glad to be done for the day. I sat back, turning in my chair, looking at the bright sky. I had found a great-sounding restaurant for dinner, and I'd checked out the tavern and planned to take Amy there afterward to listen to the live music.

I rolled my shoulders, feeling oddly nervous. I hadn't been on a date in a long time. I was partially excited, partially worried, and completely hopeful I would be kissing those full lips of hers again in a few hours. I recalled how soft they felt underneath mine, how sweet she tasted. I ran my finger over my bottom lip, remembering the way she'd nipped me then ran her tongue over the spot, soothing it. I had liked it.

A lot.

"Daddy?"

I turned at the sound of Mia's voice, shaking my head to clear it of the lustful thoughts that were creeping in.

"Hey, Sweet Pea."

She hurried over and crawled into my lap. I pressed a kiss to her head. "Finished the movie?"

"Yep."

"Dory all good?"

"Yep."

"Good."

"When are we going to Uncle E's?"

"Soon. I'll take you around four."

"How come you're not staying this time?"

"Oh." I cleared my throat, the nerves kicking in. "Daddy has a date tonight."

She scrunched up her nose. "A date?"

"Yeah."

"How come?"

I blew out a breath. "Because sometimes grown-ups like to have time with other grown-ups."

"You don't like Uncle E and Auntie Holly?"

I laughed and kissed her again. "Yes, I do. Very much. But other grown-ups are fun too. Just the same as you like playing with other kids besides your cousins."

She nodded. "Is your date a lady?"

"Yes. A very pretty one."

"Do I know her?"

"Yes. Ms. McNeil."

Her eyes grew round. "I like her."

"I like her too. So I'm taking her to dinner to give her a chance to see if she might like me too."

"And I can't come?"

"Not tonight. Maybe another time."

"Okay," she replied easily. "Auntie Holly says we're having a sleepover. Are you having one?"

I felt the heat in my neck start to build, the skin getting damp. I never expected to be quizzed by my young daughter about dating and sleepovers. I wasn't ready for this.

"No, just dinner and a music show," I explained. "But it will be late, so Auntie Holly thought it best if you sleep over. I'll come get you in the morning."

She shook her head. "We're having pancakes and going to the craft fair. You can come after lunch."

I chuckled. There were always plans when it came to Holly. "Okay, then. I'll come after lunch."

She leaned her head on my shoulder, and we sat quietly for a moment. I stroked over her dark hair, enjoying the moment with her.

"Daddy?"

"Yeah, Sweet Pea?"

"Are you gonna kiss Ms. McNeil?"

Instantly, my neck got hot again.

"Um…"

She looked up at me. "You kiss good-night on

dates. I know this." She wrinkled her nose. "I don't think I would like it, but it's a rule. So I'm not going to date for a long time."

"Good plan," I muttered.

"So, are you?"

"If it's a rule, I suppose I have to," I said with a grin.

"Just on the cheek. That's fine," she assured me.

"Got it."

She jumped from my knee. "I'm going to go get my stuff ready."

"You do that. I'll be there in a few moments to help."

She stopped at the door. "I'm a big girl, Daddy. I can do it myself."

Then she was gone.

I leaned back in my chair, chuckling.

I was pretty sure it wasn't going to be Ms. McNeil's cheek I was aiming for. But I was going to kiss her.

After all, it was the rule.

CHAPTER FIVE

SIMON

I arrived promptly at seven, unsure what to expect. Kelsey used to keep me waiting all the time. But Amy opened the door, smiling and ready.

I handed her the bouquet of flowers I had picked up for her.

"You look stunning," I said, taking her in. She was dressed in a floaty skirt, the bottom edges jagged and trimmed in lace. Her blouse hung off one shoulder, exposing her creamy skin and showing me a ladybug tattoo on her shoulder that I immediately wanted to kiss. Her hair was a mass of waves tumbling down her back, and her makeup was simple and perfect. She was artlessly sexy and beautiful.

"Thank you," she replied. "You look damn fine yourself, Mr. Fletcher. Come in while I put these in water."

I stepped inside, and she leaned in to kiss my

cheek. I couldn't resist capturing her mouth with mine and kissing her. I cupped her face, moving my lips with hers. She lifted one hand, sliding it up the back of my neck, holding me close. It took everything in me not to turn her and press her against the wall and ravish her mouth until she was whimpering in need. I pulled back, dropping another kiss to her lips, then pressed my mouth to her forehead.

"Sorry, I couldn't wait. I've been thinking about kissing you again since I left you."

She peered up at me, her lovely eyes filled with amusement.

"Don't apologize for kissing me. I liked it." She rose up on her toes and pressed her mouth to mine in a fast, hard kiss. "And I've been thinking about it too."

She walked away, the material of her skirt swaying around her ankles, her exposed shoulder showing me more of the tattoo that flowed along the top of her arm and down under her blouse. More ladybugs and butterflies decorated her skin. I stopped myself from following her to discover how far down it went on her back.

I had to adjust myself before she returned. I hadn't felt this level of desire and lust in forever.

"First date," I muttered to myself. "It's the first date, so calm down."

But so far, I was enjoying it.

It was only about a twenty-minute drive to Evansham, but it was a lovely night and the road was scenic. I loved the fact that Amy had her window partially down and the breeze blew her hair around, and she wasn't bothered by it at all. She had a soft shawl draped around her shoulders, and as the air moved through the car, I could smell her scent. Flowers and citrus, it was fresh and inviting. Soft, not overpowering.

At the restaurant, we sat at a table overlooking the water. The sun was beginning to fade, its rays reflecting on the lazy waves.

"It's so beautiful," she murmured. "Always so beautiful."

"Yes, it is," I agreed, looking directly at her.

"Stop," she insisted. "You're giving me a complex."

"You should have one. You're gorgeous."

She smiled. "Thank you. I'm glad you think so."

"Me and every other man in the room," I said.

She rolled her eyes. "I think you're exaggerating."

I chuckled as I lifted the menu. "I don't think so, beautiful."

She scoffed at my words, but I shook my head. "You are. And I like that." I indicated her tattoo. "Sexy. Sweet. Just like you."

"Oh Lord, how am I going to survive you?" she muttered.

I leaned close, taking her hand. "Hold tight. I got you."

She shook her head, but I saw her smile.

"You have to try this," I said, holding out my fork.

Amy leaned closer, and I slid the tines inside, trying not to groan as she wrapped her lips around the fork and took the tenderloin I offered her.

"Oh my God, that is so good," she mumbled. She sliced off some of her stuffed sole, and I accepted the bite, the creamy filling delicious and rich.

"Incredible," I agreed.

My nerves had disappeared as soon as I saw her earlier. Our conversations were relaxed and filled with laughter. More sharing. I swallowed the mouthful I was chewing and sat back, contemplating her. In the low light, she was even more gorgeous than before, which I thought was impossible. She was natural and easygoing. I liked her. A lot.

"Favorite time of day?" I asked.

"Evening. Once dinner is over and I'm ready for the next day, I can relax. Read. When it's still light, I can take a walk and snap some pictures or draw."

"You like to draw?"

She nodded, looking shy.

"I would like to see your work."

"I'm not a professional."

"I bet you're underestimating your talent."

"I'll show you someday."

"Soon," I replied.

"You're a little bossy, you know that?"

I shook my head. "Decisive. I have to be in my business."

"You work from home?"

"Yes. Once it was only Mia and me, I set up from home. I hired a nanny I trusted, but I was right there every day, making sure Mia got good care. As she got older, I made sure she had the opportunity to interact with other kids, and once she went to school, I got someone for a few hours a day."

"What about now?"

"I was looking, but Holly insists that Mia go home with Angela and stay there after school if need be. Otherwise, she'll come home. With the time difference to Toronto and out west, my day is a bit more flexible. I am looking for someone, though. I have meetings that are later sometimes, or I have to work long hours. I don't want to impose on Holly all the time."

"I know a few people I would recommend. One lady, in particular."

"Great. I'll get their names."

We chatted about a few other things as we finished our meal. The waiter cleared our plates and offered us a dessert menu. Amy rubbed her hands in delight. "The best part of the meal," she crowed.

I smiled widely as I looked down at the choices.

"What?" she asked.

I met her gaze. "I can't tell you how wonderful this is, Amy. I was nervous earlier. I haven't been on a date in a long time. And frankly, you are so different from the last person I dated, it's refreshing and enjoyable."

"Your ex," she said simply.

"Yes."

"Explain it to me."

The waiter reappeared, and she paused. "I can't decide between the crème brûlée or the apple crisp," she mused.

I handed my menu to the waiter. "One of each, please. Two coffees as well."

Amy smiled. "Ice cream on the crisp. Extra caramel sauce."

"Of course."

The waiter left, and I sat back, drumming my thumb on the table.

"Right there. That right there is what is so amazing about you."

"That I like caramel sauce and ice cream?"

"Yes." I scrubbed my face. "I don't want to talk about my ex or compare you, but Kelsey was fanatical about everything. Eating out with her was a nightmare once she let me see her real self." I barked a laugh. "Well, everything was eventually. But when we dated, she ate lightly, and frankly, I was too wrapped up in her, ah, assets to notice much. But she never enjoyed anything. No appetizer, never dessert, and she pushed her food around her plate, never eating much. She drank a lot of white wine, though. Later in our relationship, she criticized everything. Nothing was ever good enough for her." I looked at the table. "Mia and I certainly weren't."

Amy reached across the table, clasping my hand. "You're better off without her, then."

I met her understanding gaze, flipping my hand over and squeezing hers. "We are. But you're such the opposite. You enjoy life. You're open and real. It's refreshing and—" I ran a hand through my hair. "—I know it sounds stupid, but I find it endearing. I like you."

She smiled. "I like you too."

The waiter appeared, setting out our desserts and coffee. He left, and she picked up her spoon, holding it up in challenge and winking at me drolly. "But I love desserts, so my affection for you means nothing. I fight for the last mouthful."

I picked up my spoon, tapping it against hers.

"Duly noted. May the best man win."

She grinned. "He is going to be a she."

And we dug in.

We walked to the tavern, my arm cinched around her waist, tucking her into my side. It was a lovely night, the scent of the ocean strong in the air.

"God, I love it here," I said. "The scents and the people. The atmosphere you only get in small towns."

"I know." She hummed in agreement. "It must be

a huge culture shock coming from such a big city to Nova Scotia itself, never mind such tiny towns."

"It was and is at times. People knowing my name. The bakery remembering I like the sourdough loaf when I go in. Getting greeted by name at the pharmacy or the waves I get as I walk down the street. Everyone talking to Mia. I don't think that ever happened back there. It takes a bit of getting used to, but it's awesome. I want Mia to grow up with this surrounding her."

We entered the tavern, the noise and lights loud and bright. We found a table in the corner and ordered drinks. I tried not to laugh when Amy looked over the appetizer menu for "later."

"We might get the munchies," she explained. "I've had the nachos here. Delicious."

"Good to know."

The band came on, a lively Celtic group. The music was upbeat, fun, and loud. There was a small dance floor, and somehow I wasn't surprised when Amy pulled me to it. I wasn't much of a dancer, but I noticed no one really was. They moved to the beat, waving their arms, stomping their feet, and it was easy to get caught up in the infectious sound. The few slower songs they played, I pulled Amy into my arms and we swayed together, moving as if we'd done this hundreds of times before. She molded against me as if she was made to go there. It was an incredible high. I couldn't recall the last time I had enjoyed myself this much.

When the band took a break, so did we. The required nachos were ordered, I got Amy another drink, and I got a tonic and lime since I was driving.

She shifted her chair so we were side by side, and I draped my arm over the back, pulling her even closer.

"Having a good time?" I asked, bending close to her ear so she could hear me over the din. The tavern had gotten busier, the noise level high.

She turned her head, our eyes locking. "The best," she assured me. "This is the best date ever, Simon."

I had no choice. She was close, warm, and intoxicating. Sexy and inviting.

I had to kiss her.

So I did.

AMY

My God, the man could kiss. His full mouth felt like heaven on mine. His tongue was like sin. Sliding, stroking, teasing. Possessive and persuasive one moment, gentle and coaxing the next. He made my head spin, my body hum, and my senses explode. I wanted him more than I could ever remember wanting another man. The entire night had been foreplay. His smile and laughter, his moments of vulnerability. The intelligence and kindness that radiated from him. And for the love of all that was holy, his body. Tall, strong—

hard muscles that molded my softer curves against him. Large hands that held me tight. Hair I wanted to sink my hands into and yank as he devoured my mouth.

Then a loud thump startled us, and we pulled apart. The waitress grinned at us. "Your nachos," she said with a wink. "Save the dessert for home, eh?" She was laughing as she walked away, and I felt the heat of my blush on my cheeks.

Nevertheless, I tossed my hair back and met Simon's eyes. He wasn't at all embarrassed. In fact, he looked quite pleased with himself as he handed me a plate.

"Time to fill up the tank," he teased. "I want to dance some more, then I want to take you somewhere private and kiss you until you're groaning my name and begging me."

I leaned close, my mouth to his ear. "Begging you for what?"

He gripped my thigh under the table, his voice a low rasp. "Whatever you want. Trust me. I'll give it to you."

I had to tease him. He had wound me up tighter than a spring. I shifted closer. "Does it help to know I'm wet for you, Simon? That I've never wanted a man the way I want you?"

His grip tightened, and a shudder ran through him.

I pressed a kiss to his neck, just below his ear. "I want you to ask me for what *you* want later. I'm pretty sure it's the same as what I want. We're both going to get it."

"Jesus," he muttered. "Now I'm torn between dragging you out of here and getting you alone, or watching you eat those nachos and dance with me."

I grinned. "What's it gonna be, big boy?"

His eyes narrowed. "Eat. You're going to need it."

I took the plate. "I look forward to it."

We danced and laughed. Teased and made silent promises with our eyes. We touched and caressed, heightening the intense feeling building between us.

I had no idea who this woman was right now. I had never reacted to someone the way I was reacting to Simon. Never felt the draw, the need to have more with a man so quickly.

And I wanted more.

I wanted to feel his skin under my fingers. Slide my hands along his muscles and experience the sensation of them rippling under my touch. Wrap my fingers around his thick cock that had been pressed into me half the night. Every time we danced, I felt his desire. I wanted to see it. Touch it. Explore it with my hands and my mouth. I wanted to see what he looked like as he climaxed. How his neck muscles would bunch and stretch as his head fell back. The low, guttural noises he would make.

And I wanted to ride him, to watch his expression,

to feel his possession and passion. It simmered right below the surface, and I wanted it to explode and fill the room.

The song stopped and we clapped. Simon bent his head. "You ready to leave?"

"Yes."

He took my hand. "Let's go."

He drove past my place, and I turned to look at him.

"You missed the driveway."

He shook his head. "I'm taking you to my place. I want you in my bed and for my sheets to smell like you. Like us."

"You think we'll make it to the bed?"

He groaned. "Listen, my beauty. I have had to fight everything in me to drive. Not to pull over and take you on the hood of my car. I can't even touch you right now because I'm not sure I'll be able to stop. You keep saying stuff like that, and we won't make it in the door."

I grinned at the implied threat.

"My shoes might scratch your hood."

"Fuck the hood," he snarled.

"No, Simon," I said, leaning over, sliding my hand over the prominent bulge in his pants. "The idea is to fuck me. Not your car." I squeezed him lightly. "And I'm on birth control and clean. I know it's been a long time for you as well. I want you bare inside me."

The car accelerated, and a few moments later, he pulled up to a beautiful log home. I had no time to admire it since he was out of his door and at mine in a blink. He pulled me from the car, barely giving me a chance to take off my seat belt. His mouth covered mine, hard and desperate. His tongue was controlling, twisting with mine and leaving me breathless. He swooped me into his arms, making me gasp. He hurried to the door, carrying me as if I weighed no more than a feather.

At the door, he stopped. "It's 1962," he rasped.

"What?"

"The door code is 1962. Punch it in."

I did as he said, and the next thing I knew, we were inside, the door slamming shut with his foot, and he was carrying me up the stairs, his mouth back on mine.

There was a light burning in his room, casting a dim glow around the walls, but I had no chance to study anything. Simon set me on my feet, his breathing harsh. He stepped back.

"Are you sure you want this?"

I pulled my blouse over my head, unbuttoning the skirt so it pooled in a pile of material on the floor. I stood before him naked.

"Oh my God. You've been bare all night," he uttered in disbelief.

"I hate undergarments. I only wear them when I have to."

He shook his head. "Never wear them on my

account." He traced a finger over my collarbone, drifting it from shoulder to shoulder, then dropping his hand to one nipple, circling it.

"I'm not very—"

He cut me off. "You are exquisite." There was no doubting the honesty in his voice. The awe as he stared at me. It made me brave.

"How about you ditch the clothes?" I said, tugging on his shirt.

Seconds later, he was naked too. His torso was long and taut, the muscles evident. His arms were wide, his biceps clearly defined. His cock jutted out, thick and perfect, the head swollen and purple, already dripping for me.

Without thinking, I fell to my knees, wrapping my hand around him. Velvet over steel. Hot and smooth. Pulsating and hard.

He shuddered as he looked down. "Amy, you don't—"

It was my turn to cut him off. I licked at the head, then sucked him into my mouth.

"Jesus fuck," he muttered, resting his hand on the back of my head.

I licked and teased the crown, lapping at the length and sucking him as far in as I could. I paid attention to his noises—the low gasps, the grunts of pleasure, the hisses of delight. I gripped his ass and began sucking in earnest, hollowing out my cheeks and swallowing around him, taking even more of him in me.

He didn't disappoint with his reactions. He cursed and begged. Pleaded for more, called my name, wrapped my hair in his hand, but he never forced me. His touch was restrained, but his hips rocked in a constant motion, picking up speed, his growls coming one after the other.

"You need to stop."

"Jesus, I can't—"

"Amy, yes. Fuck, yes."

"I'm going—"

"Fuck, I can't—"

And he fell. Loudly. Wildly, his hips moving of their own volition, his movements jerky and fast. He called my name, shivered and shook, and then finally stilled, his head hanging down over his chest, his breathing hard and erratic.

I let him slide from my mouth, moving my hands to his thighs and stroking the hair-covered skin gently.

He sighed, a long, slow breath, and opened his eyes, meeting mine.

"Take the edge off?" I asked with a wink.

He bent and grabbed my elbows, dragging me up his torso. He kissed me deeply, holding me tight to his chest. He walked me back to the edge of the bed, pushing me down to the mattress.

"My turn," he said with a smirk. "Hold tight. I'm about to blow your mind."

CHAPTER SIX

SIMON

Jesus, she was beautiful. Slender, with rounded hips and a full ass that looked great in her pretty skirts. Her breasts were high and perky, not large, but molded to my hands perfectly. Her hair was wild and soft. The tattoo on her back and shoulder suited her so well. Wild flowers, ladybugs, and butterflies. She was all of that. Natural, sweet, and free.

And her mouth. Holy shit, her mouth. What she did to my cock blew my mind. And my load. I didn't want to know how she learned to do that because it didn't matter. She was here with me now, and that was where she was staying.

She lifted her arms over her head, causing her pink nipples to tip up, and they hardened under my gaze. I slowly ran my hands over her torso, cupping them, pinching and tweaking, then covering them with my mouth one at a time, sucking and licking until they were red and wet. I slipped my hand between her milky white thighs, groaning at the slick heat waiting for my touch. She gasped as I stroked her, kissing my way down her body, dropping caresses to her arms and hips, her delicate ankles and calves, then the backs of her knees as I dropped to mine in front of her, pushing her legs apart and dragging her to the edge of the mattress and close to my mouth.

She arched off the bed as I licked her center, groaning at her taste and the wetness of her. I learned what made her cry out, grasp the sheets, arch her hips closer, beg for more. I teased and licked, nibbled her clit and sucked it into my mouth, loving it with my tongue, drawing tight circles on the hard nub. I slid one finger, then two, inside her, pumping them slowly, feeling her muscles beginning to clench. I licked her harder, added a third finger, and she tightened, her voice a raspy wail as she came, flooding my mouth with her honey and gripping the back of my head, shaking and moaning her release.

I stood over her, pumping my already hard cock with my fist. I knelt on the mattress, hovering over her, then sinking inside, inch by inch, until we were flush. I wrapped her leg around my hip, staring down at her.

"You feel so incredible," I praised her. "You were meant for me."

"Oh God, Simon. Fuck me."

"Yeah? You want it hard, baby? You gonna take everything I give you?"

I scooped her up, moving with her so she was

higher on the bed. I gripped the headboard with one hand, her hip with the other, and I began to move. Long, powerful strokes. Pulling out, thrusting forward. Lifting her hips higher and changing the angle. In, out, pushing, pulling, feeling the tightness and warmth of her. Reveling in the way she clutched at my cock. Surrounded me with her wetness and need. She arched and moved, meeting my intensity with her own. Lifting her hand to grab mine on the headboard, her nails digging into my skin. I fell forward, claiming her mouth as I kept moving. Fucking her harder, going even deeper. Swallowing her cries of passion, loving how she touched me everywhere. I felt another orgasm brewing in my balls, tightening up in pleasure. I broke from her mouth, cursing and saying her name, begging her to fall with me. I shouted as it hit me, ecstasy exploding, breaking my body into bits then piecing it back together. She cried out my name, holding me tight as she milked me, taking everything I gave her, shivering, whimpering, and moaning.

Until we were sated.

Until we were still.

Then in the aftermath, I lay in her arms, cocooned and at peace. Our sweat-soaked skin melded together, the heat slowly evaporating from the air around us. I searched blindly, finding the edge of the blanket and pulling it over us, easing her into a more comfortable position. I kissed her bare shoulder, then nuzzled her neck.

"Amazing," I whispered. "You were utterly amazing."

"Not too shabby yourself," she replied, turning her head to kiss my forehead in an oddly sweet gesture. "That was beyond anything I could have dreamed."

I tucked her closer. "I plan on making all those dreams come true. Now, sleep a bit. I need you rested."

She snuggled in, and I loved how comfortable I was with her. How right this felt. I pressed another kiss to her head and let myself drift.

I was looking forward to waking up.

———

The room was silent when I woke, my bed empty. I sat up, looking around, relaxing when I spotted Amy's clothes draped over the chair. I got up and dragged on a pair of sweats, then headed to the bathroom. I chuckled at my reflection. My hair was everywhere, my lips looked as if a beautiful woman had been kissing them, and I could see a love bite on my shoulder. Another by my nipple.

My little lover was a biter. She was also passionate, giving, and loud. I was good with all of that.

I wasn't good with her being gone from my bed, though.

I finished and headed downstairs, following the dim light to the kitchen. Amy was at the island, sitting on one of the high stools. She wore my shirt I'd had on earlier, the sleeves rolled up, and she looked sexy in it. In front of her were the milk jug, an open loaf of bread, the butter dish, the peanut butter, and a jar of jam. A pile of discarded crusts was on the counter.

I sauntered toward her, trying not to laugh. Her mouth was full, and she was chewing rapidly, holding the glass of milk.

Reaching her, I grinned. "Starving?"

She nodded, her mouth still full. I tapped her cheeks. "Are you part chipmunk?"

She swallowed and took a sip of milk. "Maybe. I could nibble on your nuts later if you want."

I burst out laughing and dropped a kiss to her nose. I slid onto the seat beside her and picked up a crust. "Problem?"

"I don't like crusts with PB & J."

I tossed one into my mouth, chewing and swallowing. "Mia's favorite snack."

"Mine too." She took another slice of bread and smothered it with butter and peanut butter, added jam, cut off the crusts, and rolled it like a jelly roll.

"Mia would like it like that," I mused.

She took another large bite. "It tastes better."

I dropped another crust into my mouth, enjoying the thick peanut butter taste with the sweet jam. "Holly made the jam."

She grinned. "I know. I helped her."

She was adorable. "So, you burned a lot of

calories, did you?" I asked dryly, watching her make another sandwich.

"Uh-huh. You're a sex animal."

I smirked.

"I might be feeling a little wild again."

She paused eating. "You told me you were forty-two. Don't you need, like, some downtime or something?"

I slid off the stool and turned hers, pushing her knees apart and standing between her splayed legs. I lifted her hand, taking the last bite of her rolled-up sandwich. "When it comes to you, no. My cock thinks he is about twenty. He was ready to go for another round a while ago." I dropped my face to her neck, pushing the collar out of the way. I nuzzled her skin, smiling as she shivered and gripped my biceps.

"I like seeing you in my shirt," I growled against her neck. "I especially like knowing you're bare under it." I trailed my mouth up to her ear, sucking the lobe in and biting down. "And wet."

"So sure of yourself, are you?" she asked, a hitch in her voice.

I slid my hand under her hips, pulling her to the edge of the chair. "I bet you're so wet I could take you right here. Right now."

"In front of the milk?" she gasped, feigning shock.

"I'm going to do things to you that will curdle it."

She slipped her hands under the waistband of my sweats, tugging down the material. My cock sprang free, the height of the stool perfect to line up with her center. She was wet, hot, and so ready.

So was I.

I was surprisingly fine with defiling her in the kitchen where I ate breakfast with my daughter. I was so turned on, nothing else mattered. All I wanted, all I needed, was to be inside Amy again. To feel that rush of pleasure as she wrapped herself around me. Everything else fell away, and I lost myself with her.

Later, back in bed, I propped myself up on my elbow, gazing down at her. We'd cleaned the kitchen, had a shower, and I'd pulled her back to the mattress beside me. I wrapped a damp curl around my finger, feeling the softness between my fingers.

"Has anyone ever told you how amazing you are?" I asked.

"Stop," she hushed me.

"No. You are."

"Maybe that's postcoital glow talking."

I lowered my head and kissed her. "There is that, but it's much more. It's you. You make me feel like —Simon."

She cupped my cheek. "You don't usually feel that way?"

"Not for a long time. I'm Simon the money guy. Simon the divorced guy. Simon the single dad. Simon the responsible adult who puts everyone and everything else first." I sighed. "Tonight, I was just me. Enjoying a night out with a beautiful, sexy woman. Eating the food I like. Drinking a great glass of wine. Kissing and touching you because I wanted to. Because you wanted me to. It felt good."

Her fingers moved restlessly on my cheek. "I like just Simon," she whispered. "I like him a lot."

"Good. Because he likes you too."

I covered her mouth with mine and kissed her until she was breathless. Until my body pulsated with need for her, a steady beating rhythm under my skin that would only be satisfied once I'd had her again.

I hovered over her, staring into her fathomless eyes. "Should I stop?"

She slid her arms around my neck. "God, no. But you should come with a warning label, Simon Fletcher."

I grinned. "What warning would that be?"

"Sort of like the Energizer Bunny. Unending."

"Pleasure," I replied.

"What?" she asked, furrowing her brow.

"Unending pleasure. That's what I give."

She pulled me down, our chests melding, her skin silky against mine.

"Okay, then. Give away."

I woke in the morning later than usual. Amy slept beside me, a warm bundle of softness. Her hair was wild—a mass of golden wheat across the pillow. She faced me, her lips pursed as she slept, her arm draped over my waist. Her bare shoulders gleamed in the morning sun, her tattoo vivid on her creamy skin. I had traced that ink with my tongue. Tasted the honey of her, the sweet with the salt. I knew how thick and silken her hair felt around my hand. How she tasted— everywhere. Her incredible passion.

"Stop staring at me, stalker," she mumbled.

I chuckled. "You are too irresistible not to stare."

She opened one eye, peeking at me. "You're talking with your cock."

I laughed. "He's gifted, but talking isn't one of his strengths. He is far better at communicating in other ways."

She shifted closer. "He is talented."

I groaned as she wrapped her hand around me. "Baby, you have to be sore. I've had you four times in the past twelve hours."

"Surprisingly, I'm not."

She stroked me, her touch firm and perfect. I had no idea how I could be hard again. Feel this level of lust for this woman. But I did.

She pushed me onto my back, straddling me. I gazed up at her, the way her hair tumbled down her back. Her small, firm breasts peaked in the cool morning air. On her hip was another tattoo. A small bunch of flowers that bloomed bright colors on her skin. She was a warm, welcome weight on my thighs. She locked gazes with me as she lowered her torso and took me into her mouth again. I pressed my head into my pillow with a long hiss of pleasure.

"Jesus, woman."

"No," she mumbled, "Just Amy."

Despite the vortex of lust I was trapped in, I laughed. She chuckled, the vibration swirling around my shaft. I lifted my hips higher, needing to be deeper, closer to the sensation. The warmth.

Her thick hair tickled my thighs as she sucked and licked. She played with my balls, cupping and stroking. I was a mass of sensation, pleasure rippling through me as she took me deeper and harder. I moved under her, groaning and hissing, begging her for more. Wanting whatever she would give me. Never wanting this to end, yet desperate to feel the moment of ecstasy with her again.

She swallowed around me, and I fell. Hard, fast, unexpected. No warning or final buildup. I bellowed her name, cursed, and shook. Gripped her hair and praised her. Begged her again.

And then there was nothing. That blissful moment of peace where your body and brain disconnect and you're floating, adrift and alone.

Amy curled up beside me, and I pulled her into my arms. I pressed a kiss to her head.

"You need to come with your own warning label," I mumbled, tracing her lips with my finger. "Your mouth needs to be listed as a dangerous weapon."

Playfully, she bit the end of my finger. "Made you smile, though."

"Was that your goal?"

"You don't smile enough, Simon. I like knowing I put it on your face."

I pulled her to me and kissed her. I had no idea how to respond to those words.

I woke alone again. I could smell coffee and bacon. I got up and grabbed a quick shower, grinning at the damp towel hanging on the rack. Obviously, Amy had had a shower already and decided to make breakfast.

I showered and dressed and headed downstairs. Amy glanced over her shoulder at me with a grin.

"Morning, handsome."

"Hey, Chippy," I replied, dropping a kiss to her cheek.

"Chippy?"

"It's a short form of chipmunk. It suits you."

She rolled her eyes and handed me a cup of coffee. "Whatever. I made breakfast."

"I was going to take you out for breakfast."

She leaned against the counter, shaking her head. "You need to remember how small a town this is, Simon. They see us out for breakfast, and they'll start to talk. I don't think you're ready for that."

She turned back to the pan, and I sat down at the island. She was right. I wasn't ready for that. Despite what happened last night, we had to proceed slowly. I had to think of Mia.

I shook my head. I had barely thought of my daughter since dinner last night. My entire focus had been on Amy. The passion between us.

I watched her for a moment, so at home in my kitchen. Looking sexy in my shirt, tied around her waist in a knot, her pretty skirt flowing about her legs. She was comfortable. It felt…natural. I thought about how Mia would react. What she would think. She'd been the entire focus of my life for so long. What if she resented Amy? Didn't like her? I had to continue with caution.

It hit me that maybe I was moving too fast. That I had let last night and my frenzied lust cloud my judgment. I needed to pull back and go back to Plan A. Slow. Get to know Amy. Introduce her to Mia. Proceed from there.

I just wasn't sure how to accomplish that, given what had transpired between Amy and me.

———

My mood fractured during breakfast, my mind and heart at war with each other. I was quiet, thinking, going deep into my head. Amy seemed to sense that, as she was silent as well. We ate our breakfast, and I insisted on cleaning the kitchen. She disappeared and I heard her walk back down the stairs, but she never came into the kitchen. I wiped my hands and found her seated in the living room, staring out the window. Her usual smile was absent, but she was polite and casual as she stood.

"Can you run me home?" she asked.

"Of course," I said with a frown. "I don't expect you to walk."

She smiled and moved past me. My hands itched to touch her. To tell her the doubts and fears crowding my head. The worries. But I remained silent and followed her to the car.

The short trip was uncomfortable for both of us. I didn't know what to say, and she didn't try to fill the air with small talk. When I pulled up to her place, I began to take off my seat belt, but she stopped me.

"It's fine, Simon. I'm a big girl and can walk myself into my place."

"Amy—"

She cut me off. "It's okay," she offered. "I get it. Last night was amazing. For both of us. And it was exactly what we wanted and needed. One night. Not the start of something. I get it."

I groaned and turned my head, meeting her eyes. I saw the hurt she was trying to cover up, the pain of rejection. I shook my head. "No, Amy—"

Again, she stopped me. "Like I said, I'm a big girl, Simon. It was fun and I enjoyed myself. You take care, and I'm sure I'll be seeing you around. Maybe the grocery store again." She offered me a smile I could only describe as brittle. It was false and hid her true feelings, and I deserved the anger she was concealing.

She climbed out of the car and walked away,

never turning back. I sat for a moment, undecided, then I drove away, feeling as if I had left something behind. Something important.

I cursed myself all the way to Evan's.

But I didn't turn around.

Mia greeted me with a carefree smile and a hug when I arrived at Evan and Holly's place. She was busy with Angela and Hannah, doing some craft Holly had them involved in that they had picked up at the fair. I gratefully accepted a cup of coffee and wandered back to Evan's shop. He was at work hand-sanding a delicate-looking piece of trim, his face frowning in concentration. He smiled when he saw me, setting aside the wood and taking the cup of coffee Holly had sent him from my hands.

"Thanks, I needed a break."

I looked at the piece he was working on. "Beautiful," I offered as I ran my hand over the silken wooden top.

"It will be. My customer found it in a barn under some blankets covered in hay. I had to let it air a little and fix the warping. Now is the fun part. So much trim to fix and replicate. I'm trying to save as much as possible."

We sipped our coffee in silence for a moment. "I thought Holly would keep you inside to hear all about your date," he said finally.

I shook my head.

"Didn't go well?"

"It was great. Amy is lovely." I took a sip of coffee. "I just can't move too fast, you know?"

"I get that, but I thought you'd look happier."

I scrubbed my face. "It's complicated, Evan."

Holly walked in, carrying a plate with coffee cake on it. "How complicated?"

I met her unwavering gaze. I should have known she wouldn't accept my silence as a deterrent.

"Look, we had a great time. Amy is awesome."

"But?" she questioned.

"But what?" I countered, not wanting to have this conversation with her.

"Did you sleep with her?" she asked.

I sputtered into my coffee. "Kinda personal, Holly," I said dryly.

"Did you?"

I didn't respond.

"So, you slept with her, and that's it?" She frowned. "I'm a little shocked at your behavior, Simon. I didn't think you were a love-them-and-leave-them kind of guy."

"I have to take it slow for Mia. That's all."

"And, of course, you explained that to Amy. So she understood. You didn't leave her feeling as if she'd been used and discarded."

I felt the back of my neck break into a sweat.

"I think that's between Amy and me," I muttered.

She slammed her hands onto her hips. "She is my

friend. My best friend. If I had thought you were going to use her, I never would have encouraged her to go out with you."

"I didn't use her." I ran a hand over my eyes. "Holly, it's complicated. I like Amy. I like her a lot. But I have to take it slow for Mia. For me. Last time I tried this, I got my heart stomped on."

Her face softened. "Amy is nothing like Kelsey."

"I know. But I have to handle this my own way." I sighed. "I need to talk to Amy and clear the air. I didn't handle everything the way I should have. I panicked," I admitted.

"Why?"

I met her eyes. "Because I really liked her. And it scared me."

She stepped forward. "Sometimes in life, you have to take that chance, Simon. Evan did with me. I did with him. I knew him a few days and moved across the country with him and started a new life."

"You two are different. Special. What you have is rare, not the norm."

She smiled and cupped my face. "You deserve rare too, Simon. Trust your instincts this time. I know Amy. I know her heart. You're safe with her. What happened last time will not be repeated."

I thought about the night before. Amy's open ways. Her directness and teasing. How she made me feel. How right she felt in my arms. My bed. The way it made me smile simply to lie beside her and talk.

I shut my eyes with a groan. "I think I fucked it up."

"I'm sure you did," Holly agreed with a nod. "So figure it out and unfuck it." She strolled over to Evan and kissed him. He grinned at her, dropping another kiss to her head and whispering something in her ear that made her smile. She left, and I picked up a piece of coffee cake, biting and chewing. I met Evan's amused eyes.

"Thanks for the backup, asshole," I muttered.

He shrugged. "She's right, Simon. I know Amy. What you see is what you get. There is no hidden agenda. She is as far from being like Kelsey as you can get. If you like her, and it's obvious you do, you need to fix this and fast."

"Mia—"

He cut me off. "Stop using Mia as an excuse. She is a smart, loving kid. You bring Amy around, Mia will know she's special." He shook his head. "She wants that, you know. A mom."

I gaped at him. "What?"

"She talks to me about this stuff. To me and to Holly. She wants a family. A little brother or sister, although she'd prefer the sister. She wants a mom for her and someone for you. She knows you're lonely. My niece is pretty smart. She knows you want that too."

I was flabbergasted. Mia never said a word to me about any of this. At my confused look, Evan smiled. "She's older than her years, Simon. You know that.

She doesn't want to upset you, so she keeps it to herself."

He reached over and clapped me on the shoulder. "Figure this out. If Mia weren't in the picture, tell me, would you be here talking to me in my shop or still at home with Amy in your bed?"

"You know the answer to that."

"Then figure it out," he said.

Later that day, Mia came into our kitchen, pulling herself up onto a stool, watching as I made a simple supper. We had left Evan's place after lunch, and she had been her usual busy self, coming and going, reading, playing, and keeping occupied. She'd had a great time with her cousins but had been happy to be by herself for a while.

"Daddy?"

"Yeah, Sweet Pea?"

"Did you have fun last night on your date?"

I turned and met her serious expression. I turned off the sauce I was heating and sat across from her. "Yeah, I did."

"You like Ms. McNeil?"

"I do," I replied cautiously, wondering where this was going.

"She was nice to me when we saw her. Her eyes are kind." She wrinkled her nose. "Not like some people's. I like her smile."

I had to agree; she had a great smile.

"What are you trying to say, Mia?" I asked.

"Auntie Holly explained dating to me better than you did, Daddy. She said everyone has someone who fits them really well. Like my favorite sweater. She said sometimes you think they fit, then you find they're scratchy or the sleeves are too short, and you have to try on someone else. She says she's lucky because Uncle E fits her perfectly."

"They fit each other," I agreed. "But in this case, I have to make sure they fit you too."

"I'm not a baby, Daddy."

"I know. You're growing too fast. I don't want to upset you."

She shook her head. "I meet some kids I like, but when I get to know them, I don't want to be best friends with them. I meet others and really like them. That's sort of the same thing. If I didn't like Ms. McNeil, I would tell you. But I have to meet her first. Let her see my room and have supper with her. I can't decide if I don't know her."

I ran a hand through my hair.

When did my kid get to be so smart?

She kept talking. "If you like her, Daddy, I think I will. She's a teacher, so she must like kids, right?"

"Yes, she does."

"And she's nice?"

"Very nice."

"She likes you? You said you had to see if she did."

I thought about how we made love. How her smile made my chest warm. Her beautiful honesty.

"Yeah, she did."

"Then we should invite her to supper. Auntie Holly always invites people to supper. We could make lasagna."

I smiled. Mia and I made lasagna together. She loved to help layer it, and it was decent. I could add a salad and bread.

If Amy forgave me.

"I'll ask her."

"Okay!" She scrambled off the stool. "I have to go clean my room."

"I haven't talked to her yet, baby," I said gently.

"She'll come. I saw her watch you at Uncle E's barbecue. She smiled when she did."

Obviously, my daughter was more observant than I was.

"I see."

"And, Daddy? Stop worrying about me. I'm pretty smart."

She left the kitchen, and I laughed.

I had to agree with her again. She was far smarter than I was.

I had to figure out how to get Amy to give me another chance.

I prayed I could.

CHAPTER SEVEN

AMY

I looked around my spotless apartment, feeling partially satisfied and partially angry. It had been clean before, but now it shone—everywhere.

After Simon dropped me off, I had to do something to keep myself busy. I had no idea what happened to the open, teasing, sexy man I had spent the night with, leaving me with the withdrawn, anxious man who drove me home. A switch had flipped, and although I suspected why, I couldn't bring myself to ask him.

I was certain the passion and closeness we seemed to feel toward each other frightened him. I felt his fear, although he couldn't express it. I had hoped he would. That he would confess we had to take it slower, which I understood. But instead, he simply shut down. He dropped me off and drove away.

I was hurt by his silence and told him not to

worry. I assured him I was a big girl and knew the night was simply sex. No big deal.

Except it was.

I hadn't slept with anyone for a long time. My last boyfriend and I had broken up two years ago, and I hadn't been with anyone since then. For me, sex and emotions were entwined. With Simon, I got carried away. I thought he was feeling the same draw to me as I was to him. I was certain of it.

Perhaps I had read the signs wrong.

I had to admit, I was hurt by his almost indifference when he brought me home. He had tried halfheartedly to correct my thoughts, but not hard enough. What I had hoped was the start of something incredible was, it seemed, just a night that helped us both scratch an itch.

I shook my head, refusing to let myself get tied up in knots over someone who didn't feel the same way about me. I had been the one dumped in the last relationship, and I wasn't allowing that to happen again. Hearing Darren say I was too much for him to handle and he was tired of my free spirit and didn't love me anymore had almost broken me. It took him saying so to recognize the way he always distanced himself from me in public. I embarrassed him. After he was gone, I realized that I had tried so hard to be the woman I thought he wanted. To stop being me. Never again. I had decided then to only be myself, and if the man I was involved with couldn't handle it, I would be the one to walk away.

I hadn't expected to feel this way about Simon so quickly.

I poured a bath, filling it with my favorite floral bubble bath. I got a glass of wine, lit a candle, and sank into the warm, fragrant water. My iPhone played softly in the background, the soothing music helping me to relax.

I pushed out all thoughts of Simon and focused on deep, calming breaths. I let the water soothe, the fragrance soak into my skin, and the warmth chase away the chill I had been feeling since this morning.

Tomorrow, I was going to go and set up my classroom. Get it done so I had some days before heading back into the daily routine and be ready for the one-day open house our school always had. It was a chance for parents to bring their kids in to see the classroom and be more comfortable on their first day. It was popular with kindergarten and grade one, plus anyone moving to the area and attending the school for the first time. Smaller children enjoyed seeing their classroom and meeting their teacher, and it gave the older ones a chance to find their way around. It was this Wednesday, so I would go in and get ready, then spend the last part of summer taking some photos and walking the beach. Maybe go on a short road trip to PEI.

I mulled over what I had in storage and what I needed to go to the supply store to pick up. I needed a trip to the dollar store for some fun things. The art place for some paper supplies. I called out a list to

Siri then, satisfied, sank deeper into the water and drifted.

Simon only entered my thoughts every other moment. Other than that, my ignoring his very existence worked.

Like a charm.

The next day, I was busy in the classroom when Holly showed up. She carried coffee, smiling and looking at ease.

"Hey," she greeted me. "I thought I'd find you here."

She gave me a hug and handed me a latte. "To help restore the energy," she said with a smile.

She didn't fool me for a second. But I accepted the beverage and sipped it.

"Delicious."

"I brought cookies too."

"Great."

"I thought I could help."

"Perfect." I would never refuse an extra pair of hands. Holly often helped me—we worked well together, and she volunteered during the school year on occasion.

I showed her what I was doing, and for a while, we worked in companionable silence. I sipped my latte and munched the cookies she had baked. I never refused anything Holly made. I wasn't crazy.

Finally, I met her eyes, seeing the understanding and care in them.

I groaned. "Go ahead. Ask."

"I don't have to," she murmured. "I can see you're already upset. And you have every reason to be. Simon was an ass."

I gaped at her. I had expected her to defend him for some reason. Or tell me she warned me not to expect much from him at the start. Her next words shocked me more.

"He knows he was an asshole. He's upset with himself as well."

I wasn't sure how to respond. "He should be."

"He is." She laughed dryly. "Trust me on that one."

The words were out before I could stop them. "Is he okay?"

She smiled and came closer, rubbing my arm. "Would you care if he wasn't?"

"Yes," I admitted.

"I thought so." She drew in a deep breath. "He is a bit mixed up in the head right now, but he regrets how he acted. I know he wants to talk to you." She held up her hand before I could speak. "I am not here on his behalf or to beg you to listen to him. I'm here because you're my friend and I wanted to make sure you were okay."

"I'm fine."

"Liar," she accused affectionately.

I sat on the edge of my desk. "It was so...

amazing, Holly. *He* was so amazing. Funny and sexy. Sweet and passionate. Our night—" I paused and swallowed. "I have never experienced anything like it. It felt like a beginning."

"And then he acted like a jerk," she finished for me.

"Yes."

"Can you forgive him? Try again if he asked?"

I blew out a breath. "I don't know. Part of me wants to…"

"The girly parts, you mean?" she asked while waggling her eyebrows, looking totally ridiculous.

I laughed. "Well, those parts are willing, but I can't risk him doing this again and my getting hurt."

"I know," she said softly. "If I could say one thing?"

"Go ahead."

"Of anyone I know, Simon would be worth the risk. He told me how incredible he thinks you are. He admitted he got scared and fucked up. He regrets it."

"Does he know you're here?"

"No. I didn't come here for him. I came here for you. I just think…" She paused then rushed out the words. "I think the two of you are meant for each other."

"Pretty strong words for one date."

"Evan and I knew the first night we met."

"That's rare."

"That's exactly what Simon said," she replied with a smirk. "See, perfect."

I rolled my eyes, and she held up her hands. "Okay, I'm done. But whatever you decide, I'm here for you."

I hugged her. "Thanks."

Tuesday, I did my errands, getting everything I needed. I made another trip to the school and organized my supply closet. I looked around, pleased at the cheerful room. As always, I looked forward to the start of the year. Getting back into my routine, being with my little charges every day. I loved summer and the break, but I was ready to jump into the school year.

The next day, I gave the classroom one final inspection. I was ready. The open house would start at one and end at five. It was always a busy time, but I enjoyed it.

A rap on my door startled me, and I looked up to see Ella from Bunches of Love, the local floral shop, at my door.

"Hey, Ella," I greeted her. "What's up?"

She walked in, carrying a large vase of flowers in her arms. Bright blossoms, deep greens, and wispy grasses overflowed from the large pitcher they were in. "Delivery," she said.

"For whom?" I asked.

She smirked as she set down the arrangement. "For you." She fluffed a grass head, the wispy end dancing under her touch. "Took me a while to find everything requested for the arrangement. The sender was quite particular." She winked. "Enjoy."

She left, and I approached my desk, staring at the flowers. Daisies, asters, Queen Anne's lace, and bachelor's buttons mingled with carnations, alstroemeria, baby's breath, and tiny roses. Lacy grasses and a multitude of greens made it a stunning creation. The vase was beautiful, the mix of colors in the glazed porcelain setting off the flowers. A card was attached, and my hands shook as I stared at my name written in a bold, masculine script. I opened the envelope, reading the simple words.

> Amy,
> Regret is a small word for what I feel.
> I'm sorry is inadequate.
> A conversation is what I beg for.
> Please.
> Yours—Simon.

I touched a soft petal, stroking the velvety texture. All the flowers were my favorites I had listed at dinner. He had listened and remembered. Gone to a great deal of trouble to get them for me. It occurred to me that he had ordered them from the local florist, not a nearby town. Although Ella wasn't a gossiper, I knew a few of her staff liked to talk among themselves. They would notice this unique arrangement and who sent it to me. It might start unwelcome chatter about us.

Except there was no *us*—was there?

I reread the card. *Yours—Simon.*

Was he mine? Did he want to be? Did I want to talk to him?

I rubbed my eyes. I *did* want to talk to him. To find out why. Have him explain to me what happened.

But was I ready for it? Was he?

I picked up my phone and sent him a text.

AMY

Simon, Thank you for the flowers.

They are beautiful.

Busy at school with the open house.

Perhaps a conversation can happen after it is done.

I had hardly set the phone down when it buzzed with a reply.

SIMON

Amy,

Not as beautiful as you.

When you're ready, if you'll listen, I'd like to talk.

I'll wait.

I smiled at his words, unsure how to reply, then decided it was best not to. I had to concentrate on the task at hand. Simon and his pretty flowers would have to take a back seat for the time being.

It was a busy, productive afternoon. I met some of the children who would be in my classroom, talked with the families, sat with the little ones and did an easy craft so they would be excited to come back. I answered questions, soothed the nerves of a few parents and children alike, and thoroughly enjoyed the time I spent with them. My heart had raced when a familiar set of shoulders walked past my door, the deep cadence of Simon's voice catching my ear as he led Mia toward her classroom. I should have known he'd be there. It was Mia's first time attending this school, and he was very involved in her life.

He glanced over his shoulder, and for a second, our eyes locked. He said so much with one brief look that it stopped me, and I stared after him, feeling off-kilter. It took me a moment to find my voice again and carry on acting as if everything was normal.

The flowers on my desk were admired, most people thinking I had brought them in to brighten the room. The sender and the reason, I held close to my heart. I smiled at the compliments and never elaborated.

The afternoon wound down, the halls emptying and the building getting quiet. I tidied the classroom, putting away the craft supplies, smiling as I cleaned up glitter and markers, glue and paper bits. It was rare I allowed glitter in the classroom since it got everywhere, but today was a special day. I stood, ineffectually wiping down my skirt, when a soft knock made me look up.

Framed in my doorway was Simon. In front of him, Mia stood, small and sweet, smiling at me. Simon looked nervous, his anxiety showing as he gripped the edge of the doorframe and waited for me to speak. Our eyes locked, emotions flowing between us in a silent river of unspoken words. I stood, clearing my throat.

"Hello."

Mia bounded in, happy and at ease. "Hi, Ms. McNeil!"

I crouched in front of her, meeting her eyes. "Hello, Mia. Did you enjoy your introduction to your classroom and the school?"

She bobbed her head. "It was terrific! I met some new kids, and we're gonna be great friends—I just know it," she enthused. "I liked my teacher, Mrs. Reynolds, too. They never did this at my old school. It's awesome."

"I'm glad you had a good time."

"I know where the lunchroom is and the bathroom. I won't have to worry about it now."

I nodded in agreement. Kids settled better if some of the unknown was removed. I liked the idea of the open house for the day.

Simon followed her in, standing behind her as she spoke. I rose to my feet. "Hello, Simon."

"Amy," he replied. "I hope your day was a good one?"

"Busy."

"I see the glitter has been out."

I grimaced. "Only for today. It gets everywhere."

Mia giggled. "Daddy says he farts glitter when I use it."

I felt my eyes widen, and a burst of laughter left my mouth. "Is that right?"

His eyes crinkled, joining me in my amusement. "I swallow enough of it. It does seem to settle everywhere—including the bottom of my coffee cup."

"I see."

For a moment, the room was silent, and Simon ran a hand through his hair, looking nervous and unsure.

"So, Mia and I made dinner for tonight. Our specialty."

"Lasagna!" Mia added.

I smiled. "How nice."

"We, ah, we were wondering, since you were busy all day and everything, if you'd like to join us."

"Join you?" I repeated, surprised.

"For supper," Mia interjected, looking between us as if we were inept. "You had a date, and you liked Daddy and he liked you, so now you have to come for supper and see if we all like each other. I told Daddy he was silly—I already like you. You smile with your eyes."

I tried not to laugh at Simon's horror at Mia's word vomit. The tips of his ears turned pink, and he looked more uncomfortable than earlier, which I didn't think was possible.

"Mia," he admonished. "That was private."

She shrugged, not at all put out. "You said it, Daddy. And you never said it was a secret. I'm not a mind reader."

This time, I did laugh. She was direct and honest. I liked the fact that Simon had talked to her about me. And maybe dinner with the two of them was a good idea. Then Simon and I could talk.

I bent down again. "That would be a big treat, Mia. I love lasagna."

"Daddy and I make the best. I help with the layers, and he says I do a great job." She smiled widely. "And we always have garlic bread. I love garlic bread," she added in a low voice.

"Me too."

She clapped her hands. "So, you'll come?"

I straightened, meeting Simon's eyes. He was watching us closely, waiting for my response.

"Yes."

He visibly relaxed, his shoulders dropping, his smile easier. "Can we walk you out?"

I shook my head. "I have to tidy a bit more, and I want to stop home and drop off my flowers and change." I smirked. "I wouldn't want you farting glitter because of me."

He chuckled. "We can help."

Mia headed to the flowers, investigating them as I stepped closer. "People would see, Simon. Probably not a good idea. I'll come once I'm finished and go home and change."

He captured my hand, pressing it close to his chest. "That's fine, Amy. But know one thing. I don't care if they see. If they talk. After tonight, they're going to see us together a lot."

"Is that a fact?" I murmured, my voice calm even as my heart rate picked up at his words.

"Yes, it is," he said firmly.

"I think you're jumping the gun."

He glanced at Mia and stepped closer, my hand still trapped on his chest, his scent drifting around us. "I gave us some space. Time for you to decide if you could forgive me and time for me to make sure my head was on right. The bottom line is, the gun has gone off, Amy. I'm going to lay it on the table tonight and apologize until you believe me. And then we're going to move forward."

I blinked. "I see."

He pressed a kiss to my cheek. "Finish here and come to me. I'll be waiting."

Then he called to Mia. "Come on, Sweet Pea. Let's go. We have to go to the bakery and then head home and put the lasagna in the oven. Ms. McNeil is hungry."

"Okay," she agreed and hurried over.

"See you soon," he said as he took her hand, and they walked out the door.

"Daddy." I heard her say as they headed down the hall. "Were you holding her hand?"

"Yep," he replied.

"Is that like kissing? A date thing?"

"Sort of."

"Are you going to do that a lot?"

I leaned out the door to hear better. Simon glanced over his shoulder, spying me. He winked.

"Every chance I get."

"Okay."

They disappeared around the corner.

I leaned against the doorframe, suddenly breathless at the thought of being kissed by Simon again.

I shook my head. We were going to talk. Not kiss.

At least, that was what I told myself.

CHAPTER EIGHT

AMY

I felt nervous as I pulled up to the front of Simon's house. I sat in the car, admiring the pretty log cabin, taking in details I hadn't seen the night he'd brought me here. The wraparound porch with a large swing set in the corner. The flagstone pathway leading to the front entrance. The beautiful copper lights on either side of the door that welcomed you. The rich patina of the logs and the cedar accents. The house had been built to take advantage of the view of the ocean from all angles. A garage was set off to one side, not interfering with the scenery. The grass was green and dark. It needed some flowers in the front, some pots on the porch—otherwise, it was my idea of the perfect house.

I slid from the car, lifting the box I had brought with me from the bakery. I knew Simon had bought bread, but since he liked dessert as much as I did, and I had a feeling Mia did as well, I decided to bring something else to add to the dinner. I had picked up one of Marie's famous fudge brownie cakes. Thick, dense, and fudgy, it was addictive and one of my favorites. I was lucky she still had one in the display case when I arrived.

The front door opened, and Simon appeared on the porch. My breath caught at the sight of him. He had changed into a Henley and jeans. The shirt hugged his torso and arms, and his jeans molded to his legs. He had a tea towel tossed over his shoulder, and his hair was ruffled as if he'd run his hands through it a hundred times. He hurried down the steps to meet me, smiling and looking relieved.

"I didn't think you'd show up."

"I told Mia I would." I handed him the box. "I brought dessert."

He took the box and stepped closer. "Thank you."

I was caught in his intense gaze. "You're-you're welcome," I sputtered out.

He moved closer, the warmth of his body soaking into mine. "I'm sorry, Amy. I'm so sorry." He lifted my hand to his mouth, pressing a kiss to my palm, then holding it to his cheek. "I have so much to say and so many apologies to make, but I need to start off with that."

"Why?" I whispered, even though I knew we couldn't get into it with the chance that Mia would appear at any moment.

"I panicked. I shut down. I acted like a complete asshole. I wanted to turn around and come to your place and explain, but I…" He shook his head. "I was an idiot."

"Yes, you were." Then I pressed my hand into his cheek, feeling the roughness of his whiskers on my skin. "But I understand."

He smiled. "Of course you do. You understand so much more than I gave you credit for."

"We have to talk though. I can't do that again. It hurt, Simon."

"I know and I'm sorry. I never meant to hurt you and I hate that I did. I wasn't sure you'd even speak to me again after the way I shut down."

"If it happens again, I'm done."

"It won't." He drew in a deep breath. "Once Mia goes to bed, we'll talk, and I'll tell you everything. You can decide if you forgive me, and we'll figure it out."

The words were out before I could stop them. "I do forgive you."

He covered my hand with his. "Amy," he breathed out.

"But we have to talk," I repeated. "I can't put myself out there and have you reject me again."

He bent his head, pressing his mouth to mine. It was soft, gentle, and sweet. "I won't," he promised. "We'll talk until I know you're certain." He kissed me again, this time his lips lingering.

Until a voice from the porch broke us apart. "Daddy! You kiss at the end of the date! I told you that!"

"Oops," I mumbled against his mouth.

"Oops, indeed. Caught kissing my woman by my daughter in broad daylight before the date has even started."

I stepped back. "For shame, sir."

He grinned. "I'd call it worth it." He linked our hands. "Come inside. Prepare to be Mia-fied."

I allowed him to lead me. I liked how my hand felt held tight in his.

As if it belonged there.

The house smelled incredible. The table was set, and Mia was excited. She tugged my hand, and I followed her around as she showed me the house. Simon strolled behind us, making the occasional comment.

"This is Daddy's office. He plays on the computer all day."

"Yep," he said with a dry laugh. "Me and FreeCell all day."

"You should try Toon Blast or something. Branch out," I teased.

"Good advice."

I saw the family room, the guest rooms, had a long tour of Mia's room, including her beloved bookshelves and toys. It was a girly room with lots of pink and lace. Stuffed animals were stacked in the corners. A small table was set up by the window. It held a large cup of coloring pencils and a stack of paper. Pretty curtains fluttered in the breeze.

"Holly helped with the room," Simon muttered.

"It's perfect."

The tour ended as we passed the door at the end of the hall. Simon's room. Mia waved her hand. "Daddy sleeps there." She skipped ahead. "It's boring."

Simon leaned close, his breath hot on my neck. "Not all the time. Not when you're in there with me."

I had to swallow at the sudden dryness in my throat. He chuckled.

I followed Mia back to the kitchen. I slipped onto one of the barstools and accepted the glass of wine Simon slid my way. He removed the bubbling lasagna from the oven and put the garlic bread in to heat. Mia sat beside me, chatting. She talked about her cousins and Holly, excited about the fact that I knew them. She talked about her uncle E, her affection for him evident.

"He sent me presents every year since I was born. I only met him a few months ago, but I love him."

"Evan is a special man," I agreed.

She nodded. "His sister is my mom, but she doesn't like us. I don't know her, and that's okay. Daddy explained she doesn't like anyone very much— even herself, which is sad. I like me. Daddy likes me. We have our own family. Do you have a family, Ms. McNeil?"

Her words make my chest ache. She stated them so matter-of-factly. But I smiled at her.

"I think outside school, you can call me Amy, okay?"

She nodded.

"My parents live in Halifax, where I grew up."

"Do you have sisters or brothers?"

"One brother. He's older than I am."

"Does he have kids?"

"No. He travels a lot."

"I want a brother or a sister. Maybe both. But Daddy says we have to wait."

I met Simon's eyes across the room where he was leaning against the counter watching us.

"Wait?" I replied.

She nodded. "We have to have a mommy to have babies. Do you want babies, Amy?"

Simon cleared his throat. "Mia, that's personal."

"I'm just asking, Daddy."

"I would like children, yes," I replied.

"Do you like little girls?" she asked.

I realized she was interviewing me in her own way. Her eyes reminded me of Simon's. Anxious, waiting for my reply.

"I love little girls," I assured her.

"Daddy says I'm smart and well-behaved."

"Most of the time," Simon interjected.

"None of us is perfect," I replied. Then I looked down at Mia. "I agree with your daddy. You are smart. And I like you, Mia."

She beamed. "I like you too." She jumped off her stool. "I'm going to wash my hands for supper."

She rushed off, and Simon leaned on the counter. "I think you passed," he said dryly. "Sorry."

I shook my head. "Don't be. She can ask me things. It's fine."

"You're good with her."

"I like kids. I love talking to them and hearing their thoughts. Their process fascinates me."

He leaned closer. "You fascinate me."

I picked up my wine. "Stop it."

"I mean it."

Mia reappeared, skidding to a halt. "Daddy, why are you so close to Amy? Are you trying to kiss her again?"

"Wouldn't dream of it," he replied. "She was talking really quietly, so I had to lean close to listen."

"Hmmph."

The timer rang on the oven, and Simon winked. "Saved by the bell. Dinner is ready, my ladies. Go sit down, and I'll bring it in."

I curled up on the sofa, waiting for Simon. Dinner had been delicious. Simon made a great lasagna, and I made sure to admire the layers Mia helped with. The garlic bread was soft and the cake a huge success. It felt oddly intimate sitting in the dining room with them, listening to their conversations and laughter, joining in when I could. It felt like being part of a family. After dinner, I helped clean up, and then Simon ran a bath for Mia and she asked if I would read to her. I picked a book and sat at the little table with the book open on it. Simon sat beside her on the bed, and she laid her head on his lap as she listened, falling asleep surprisingly fast. Before climbing into bed, she had stopped by the table.

"Thank you for the cake, Amy. And for coming. Will you come again?"

"I would like that."

She flung her arms around my neck, and I hugged her hard. She was warm and sweet-smelling from her bath. She snuggled into my embrace, and I held her close, feeling strangely emotional as I did. I wanted to tuck her in. Stroke her hair. Sing to her. I had the feeling she wanted that as well.

But she drew back and kissed my cheek. "I like you," she whispered. "Daddy does too. Please come back."

Then she headed to her dad, leaving me feeling warm and wanted.

I'd slipped from the room as Simon tucked her in and waited for him downstairs. When he appeared, he sat beside me, taking my hand.

"Thanks. She liked that."

"Not a problem. I enjoyed it."

He sighed. "I'm a package deal, Amy."

"I know that. I knew it the day I met you."

"My ex did a number on me. She shook my confidence. All I was to her was a cash cow. All Mia was to her was a way to keep getting money."

"You're way more than that."

He turned to me. "You made me feel that way. You made me feel as if you saw me."

"I do see you. I don't like you because you have money, Simon. I'm not built that way."

"I know."

"What happened the other morning?"

He took my hand. "I swore I would never get myself in the position of letting my heart get broken again. I swore I would take it slow. But with you, there is no slow, Amy. It scared me. One dinner, one night with you, and I was seeing forever. Seeing you in my kitchen, in my bedroom, except it was *our* kitchen, *our* bedroom, *our* home. I hadn't even introduced you to Mia. Seen how the two of you interacted. She has to come first, and I was falling for you without even thinking of her. It shocked me."

"And you pulled back."

"Like an idiot, yes. Trust me, Holly reamed me well. So did Evan. I retreated when I should have advanced. I should have told you how I was feeling."

"My last boyfriend shut me out. Then walked away after he told me I was too out there for him. He was tired of my bohemian ways and the fact that I was different from other women. He was embarrassed to be seen with me. It hurt."

He shook his head, pulling my hand to his chest. "That's what draws me to you, Amy. I like your openness, your honesty, and your way of looking at things. My ex-wife was cold. Removed. She walked away from Mia without a glance. Divorced me without a thought. I like how you see me. How you act with my daughter. I want to explore this with you. I want you to try with me." He paused. "If you can forgive my actions and want to."

"You won't pull away again?"

"No. I was an idiot. But I'm a fast learner, and it won't happen again. Frankly, the thought of you not in my life is unacceptable. You make me feel—" He stopped, then shrugged and smiled. "As corny as it sounds, I feel complete."

His quiet confession thrilled me. "Then, yes."

"Thank God."

And his mouth was on mine.

A lifetime passed with Simon's lips working my mouth. He kept me close, our bodies melded together as we lost ourselves to the passion of the moment. Everything was amplified. His touch, his taste, his scent soaked into my senses, forever imprinting themselves in my mind.

We broke apart, our eyes locked. His gaze was hooded and dark. He dragged his thumb over my lips.

"Jesus, Amy, I want you."

I opened my mouth, and he shook his head. "I know we can't. I can't rush you. I have to prove myself."

"You have proven yourself. You introduced me to Mia."

"I want to introduce you to everyone. As mine."

I felt my eyes widen. "Slow your roll, Romeo."

His voice was low and raspy. "I told you—with you, there is no slow." He drew in a deep breath. "With Kelsey, I constantly had doubts, made excuses for her in my mind. With you, all I feel is a rightness. You fit with Mia and me so well." Then he frowned. "But wait, how are you feeling about this? Being involved with a man with a child? Being involved with my child? I mean—"

I cut him off, placing a finger over his lips. "Mia is a joy. I want to get to know her and you better. I know this isn't a conventional relationship, Simon. That if we progress, I would become her, ah, step—"

He shook his head, this time silencing me. "You would become her mom, Amy. I already know your heart. There would be no step in anything. For either of you. We would be a family."

His words brought tears to my eyes. "How do you feel about adding to that family?" I asked.

"As in having more children with you? Sign me up, Chippy. I'll practice getting you pregnant until we get it right."

I laughed at him. "Can we take this one step at a time, Simon? Yesterday, I thought we were done. Today, you're going a million miles an hour."

He sobered and sat up, pulling me onto his lap. "I'm just laying it out there, Amy. I'm not looking for casual. I can't do casual with you. You make me feel too much. I see a future, and I want you to know that."

"I do. And frankly, I want it too. But we need to make sure we're thinking clearly and include Mia in all of this."

He smiled and bent his head, kissing me. "That right there proves my point."

I snuggled into his chest, and he leaned back, holding me close.

"I want you to stay," he urged after a few moments of silence.

"Mia—"

"Sleeps like the dead. She'll be up by seven, but you can leave before. I just want to hold you tonight."

There was nothing I wanted more than to stay and be held by Simon. To wake up with him wrapped around me, safe and warm in his arms.

"Just to hold me?" I repeated.

"Well, I can try," he admitted.

I laughed quietly, already feeling his lack of success. I shifted on his lap, and he hissed.

"If you keep moving, my efforts will be in vain," he protested.

"Shut up and take me to bed."

Moments later, I was naked and under him. His skin slid against mine, our bodies moving as if they'd known each other for decades. Our hands caressed and touched. Our mouths pressed together, muffling the groans and whimpers, keeping our coupling private. He settled between my spread legs, burying himself inside me and taking me hard. Hitting that spot only he had ever discovered. He thrust powerfully, my orgasm sweeping over me fast. I screamed into his mouth, shaking and thrashing under him. He broke away, his hot mouth at my ear. "You're going to give me another one, Amy. Then I'm going to come, and you're going to join me. You hear me?"

He slipped his hand between us, toying with my clit. I arched at his touch, another pinnacle bearing down on me quickly. I tightened around him, and he chuckled against my throat, biting lightly at the juncture of my neck.

"Now with me," he groaned, moving faster, pinning me to the mattress, his fingers and cock working in tandem.

"I can't," I whimpered.

"Oh, baby, you can," he replied, suddenly rearing back and pulling me up his thighs, his cock sliding in deeper and sending me spiraling into another dimension.

He got what he wanted. I clapped my hand over my mouth as I climaxed. He cursed and groaned low in his throat, riding me until he was done. His orgasm was a sight to see. His head fell back, his muscles taut and flexing as he pumped his hips, filling me. He shuddered, then stilled, his head sinking to his chest.

"Fuck," he muttered.

I sighed, my body exhausted after three intense orgasms. I ran my hand over his torso.

"Yeah," I agreed. "Wow."

Then he lifted his head, his eyes dancing. "See—no control."

"Set the alarm," I reminded him, my eyes beginning to close.

He rolled over, pulling me into his arms. I heard him mumble to Siri, and I was out.

CHAPTER NINE

AMY

The next morning, I woke up, looking around in panic. It was still early, but the alarm hadn't gone off. With a low curse, I flung off the heavy arm trapping me and slid out from under the covers. I grabbed my clothes, pulling them on as Simon sat up, watching me, confused.

"Your alarm didn't work."

"Shit," he muttered, sliding from bed. He opened his door, peering into the hall. "She's still asleep. Her door is closed."

"Okay."

We crept down the steps, pausing by the door. He pulled me in for a kiss. "Why do I feel like a teenager about to be caught by my parents?" he whispered.

"Your parents would be easier to handle than—"

My words were cut off by Mia's excited voice.

"Where are you going?"

We turned as one, staring at the pajama-clad figure standing by the kitchen island.

"Um," I began, unsure what to say.

"I have the pancake stuff ready," Mia said. "Auntie Holly always makes pancakes for sleepovers."

"What?" Simon asked.

She stepped forward. "I got up and saw Amy in your bed, so I know you had a sleepover. Auntie Holly always says sleepovers are fun times and deserve pancakes, so I got the stuff out."

Fun times? That was one way to describe it.

"I thought you were still asleep," Simon replied, running a hand through his hair.

"I shut my door because Mr. Bear was still sleeping. But I'm up." She looked at us quizzically. "Don't you want pancakes? Wasn't your sleepover fun?"

I burst out laughing, because there was nothing else to do. Fun times had been had aplenty. I'd stayed, and we'd made love again, with Simon's wandering hands finding me in the night two more times. In trying to sneak out, we'd been busted.

And now we had to have pancakes to celebrate that.

I dropped my purse. "I love pancakes. And it was pretty fun. Your daddy snores, though."

Mia's eyes widened. "I know!"

"Hey," Simon protested. "I don't snore."

"You can sleep with me next time. Or in the guest room. I guess Daddy was too lazy to make up the bed." She shook her head. "He hates making the bed."

I tried not to laugh again. She was adorable and funny.

Simon huffed under his breath. "She sleeps with me when she's here. That's the rule."

"I don't get much sleep with you. Maybe the guest room is a good idea," I teased, keeping my voice low.

"I don't think so," Simon growled.

I met his dancing gaze. He was thrilled we'd been busted. In fact, I wondered if he had set an alarm at all. I narrowed my eyes, and he grinned. He was never going to admit it, even if the sneaky man had planned this.

"You do snore," I said, just to piss him off.

"Yes, you do," Mia agreed. "Big snores, Daddy."

"Whatever," he muttered. He leaned close and kissed my ear. "You make noises too. But those ones I like."

I slapped him away and took Mia's hand. "Do you like peanut butter on your pancakes?"

"Peanut butter?" she repeated. "With syrup too?"

"Yep."

"Oh, can I try, Daddy?"

He scratched his head. "Peanut butter and syrup? That seems a little weird to me."

"Don't knock weird until you've tried it."

"Yeah, Daddy," Mia quipped. "You always tell me I have to try it before I decide I don't like it. I think it sounds nummy."

He threw up his hands. "Fine. We'll try it."

I grinned. "Good answer."

"Sure, sure. Whatever makes my girls happy."

That made me smile. And as I walked into the kitchen, I had a feeling today was the start of my future.

Simon, Mia, and me.

First day of school, I was up early and in my classroom, making sure everything was ready. The past while had flown by. I'd spent more time with Simon and Mia than anywhere else. More time at their house than my apartment. In fact, I hated leaving them, my little space now feeling empty when I was there. Lonely.

When I was at Simon's place, I was now part of the nighttime routine. Reading to Mia, both Simon and me on her bed, her cuddled between us. I helped her with her bath, brushed out her long hair. Showed her a fancy braid I liked to do. I loved her good-night kisses, morning snuggles, and how she just accepted me as me. Simon tried not to laugh the day she came downstairs wearing a bandanna in her hair like mine and boots on her feet with her skirt. He told her she was adorable and kissed her. Then he did the same to me. I was Chippy to Simon; she was Sweet Pea. I loved how she called him Daddy.

He loved it when I did the same thing, but for an entirely different reason.

Last night when I insisted I had to go home, both Simon and Mia were disappointed. But I needed to get some rest and be prepared for today. I hated driving away from them, even if it was only across town. I missed them right away.

I thought about Simon's mutterings from last night while I straightened already perfectly lined-up chairs and triple-checked the snacks I had ready.

"You should just give up your place."

"I have a lease," I responded.

"Break it. Sublet it. I'll cover it. I want you here. So does Mia. The place is just a house when you're gone."

"And what is it when I'm here? A submarine?" I laughed.

"A home," he said simply, his words honest and steady.

It took all I had not to tell him yes.

"Slow," was all I said, even though my heart rejoiced at his sweet words.

We hadn't even been out in public much. Not in the town, really. A few dates at out-of-the-way places, spending time with Holly and Evan. But mostly, it was the three of us. We explained to Mia what private meant and promised her that soon she could tell people, but right now, it was something to be kept between us.

Her eyes had widened. "Like a family secret? Like Uncle E and Auntie Holly expecting another baby?"

Simon and I had glanced at each other in shock. We didn't know that.

"How do you know that?" Simon had asked.

"Angela told me. Because I'm family," she explained.

"Yes. Like a family secret," Simon said. "When we say it's okay, you can tell people."

"Okay," she agreed happily. "I like having a family secret of my own."

I shook my head, hearing the sounds of the halls beginning to fill. I needed to concentrate on some other children today. I hurried to the door and began to welcome my little charges.

SIMON

Impatiently, I waited outside for Mia. I had walked her into her classroom today, but parents were to wait outside at the end of the day. I hoped her first day had been a good one.

Holly appeared beside me, smiling. "Hey."

"Hey, you," I replied and wrapped my arm around her waist for a hug. "How are you?"

"Good," she replied.

"I hear more than good," I said with a wink.

She laughed. "Family secrets being spilled, are they?"

"Yep."

"We were going to tell you this weekend. Angela knows because Evan gets excited about babies."

"Can't say I blame him. But, ah, didn't he have a vasectomy?"

She shrugged. "He was one of the rare cases, and it failed. We found that out when I miscarried last year. I didn't even know I was pregnant at the time. He was going to have it redone, but we decided not to. And this time, all seems to be well, and we'll have another baby soon."

"Congratulations."

She hip checked me. "Think you'll have one of those in your future?"

"I think I'll have a lot of things I didn't expect."

"Good," she replied. "You deserve it."

The doors opened, and Mia came out, looking for me. I bent and caught her as she raced toward me, filled with news of her day. Holly and I listened, Angela arriving as well, happy and excited to see us.

I glanced up and met Amy's eyes across the sidewalk. She was with the few children left to be picked up, cheery and talking to them. She smiled in my direction, then returned her attention to her small group. I watched her, the tug in my chest growing stronger the longer I stood there.

It hit me that she didn't expect me to cross the cement and acknowledge her. She expected me to keep our relationship hidden still. Except, there was no need to. She wasn't Mia's teacher. We were free to date.

I recalled the way her ex had shunned her. Was

embarrassed by her. Wanted to tamp down her free spirit and beautiful, open soul. Make her a carbon copy of some of the women standing around waiting to pick up their kids, with their perfectly coiffed hair, bored expressions, and discontentment written in their eyes.

The last child Amy was waiting with ran over to his father, laughing as he was swooped into a big hug. The dad waved at Amy, who smiled and waved back. She paused as if unsure what to do next, lifting a hand to her hair and smoothing it into place. For a moment, I caught a flash of her vulnerability. She looked so alone and unsure. Then her face became pleasant and smooth.

I turned to Holly. "Excuse me."

She grinned. "Go claim her, tiger."

I took Mia's hand, and we headed in Amy's direction. She saw us coming, and her eyes grew wider as we approached. I swung Mia into my arms as I stood in front of Amy. I bent and kissed her cheek.

"Hey, Chippy," I said loudly. "How was your first day back, love?"

She blinked.

I kissed her again, this time pressing my mouth to hers.

"I missed you. You and Mia."

"Oh," she breathed out. "Simon, what—"

I interrupted her.

"Mia and I want to hear all about it. And she can

hardly wait to tell you about hers. I thought I'd take my girls out to supper. You up for that?"

"Supper?"

"Yeah. Out. Unless you want to get takeout and head home? I could rub your feet."

"Home?" she repeated quietly.

"With us. Where you belong," I said just as quietly.

"I'd love some pizza."

"Out it is, then."

"But after…" She let the words trail off, her meaning clear.

"Home," I stated.

She nodded. "I need to get my purse and tidy the classroom."

"I'll wait."

She leaned closer. "People are looking."

I shrugged. "Let them look. I have nothing to hide. I'm here to pick up my daughter and my girlfriend."

Her eyes were like saucers. "Okay, then. But I need a little time."

I winked. "We can help."

"No, it's fine. Like ten minutes."

"I'll be waiting."

"We'll be waiting, Daddy," Mia corrected me.

"That's right. *We'll* be waiting."

Amy's smile was brighter than the sun on an August afternoon. Its warmth hit my chest and made me smile with her.

"Okay," she breathed out and hurried away.

I glanced at Holly, who gave me a subtle thumbs-up. I met a few curious gazes with a calm smile and then ignored the rest.

I made Amy happy with a simple gesture. I made Mia happy.

And they, in turn, made me happy.

Meeting Amy had brought me an unexpected gift. A second chance at love. I hadn't said the words yet, but I felt them. And I planned to tell her how I was feeling later when we were alone.

I loved her, and she brought me joy. I wanted that feeling forever.

I was grabbing it with both hands.

And I planned to never let it go.

CHAPTER TEN

AMY

I headed to my classroom and made sure I was ready for morning. Normally, I would spend some time prepping, but I was ahead for the week and I had cleaned as the day went, so it didn't take long. I grabbed my purse from my desk and headed back toward the doors.

One of the other teachers was walking toward me, and I straightened my shoulders. Eleanor Aldridge and I didn't get along. Even though she was only a few years older than I was, we were vastly different. She wore baggy clothes, and her hair was always pulled back in a tight bun. She was rigid and strict, a stickler for rules, and she felt I was too "out there," with my wardrobe, thoughts, and ways of teaching. I, in turn, felt she had too heavy a hand for third graders, but she insisted they needed to be kept in line. My arguments that they were children for such a short time was met with a roll of her eyes and derision. We usually stayed clear of each other.

I forced a smile to my face. "Eleanor. Good first day?"

She pursed her lips. "I have some troublemakers in my class. I'll set them straight quickly."

I barely managed to hide my eye roll. I felt bad for the "troublemakers." I wondered if they had the audacity to laugh or act like kids in her class.

"Wow," I murmured. "First day and in trouble already."

She crossed her arms. "I witnessed the spectacle outside earlier."

I frowned. "Spectacle?"

"Kissing a student's father. Showing off in front of everyone." She shook her head. "Very unprofessional. I'm surprised you haven't been reprimanded."

I mimicked her stance and crossed my arms. "There are no rules about dating the parent of a student not in your class. Principal Bremmer has been notified that we are dating and has no issue with it. As for the spectacle, as you call it, my students were all picked up and I was done for the day, so I did nothing unprofessional. I highly doubt anyone else would consider a kiss hello scandalous."

"Not wise to mix your professional life with your personal life."

I drew back my shoulders. "My personal life is none of your concern, and I don't appreciate nor welcome your thoughts."

MELANIE MORELAND

She sniffed. "It's everyone's concern when it affects the school. Favoritism is frowned upon."

"My relationship with Simon doesn't affect the school at all. I don't teach Mia, so there is no favoritism." I waved my hand. "If you have a problem, take it up with the principal. I have no desire to listen to you anymore."

"I'll be watching you," she warned.

It was impossible to hold back my laughter. "You do that, Eleanor. Watch away when you're not dealing with your troublemakers."

I walked away, shaking my head. I refused to let her dampen my spirits. Outside, I found Simon and Mia waiting, talking to Holly. I walked toward them, meeting Simon's warm gaze.

Holly grinned at me. "We're joining you for pizza."

I linked my hand with Simon's, returning her grin. "Great. The more, the merrier."

She laughed. "We'll meet you there. Half an hour?"

"Sounds good."

"Dad, can I go with Angela and Auntie Holly?"

"If you want."

I watched as he strapped her in the back with Angela and waved them off, blowing kisses. He was affectionate with his daughter, which I loved seeing.

He turned to me. "I guess I didn't think this through very well. You have your car."

112

"I do. But I'll follow you to your place, and we can head to the restaurant together. I'll go home from there later."

"Sounds good."

Eleanor exited the building, walking to her car. She glared at us the entire way, making Simon frown.

"Isn't that one of the teachers?"

"Yes. She teaches the other grade three class. Thank goodness Mia didn't get her as a teacher," I muttered as she drove away, hands on the wheel at ten and two, and checking the lane opening three times. She pulled out carefully and drove away slowly.

"Is she mad at you or something? What was the look for?"

I sighed, leaning against my car. "She and I don't see eye to eye over children—or anything, really. She's strict and uptight. Runs a very regimented classroom. Thinks I'm flighty. Informed me I was unprofessional earlier, and I shouldn't be dating you."

"What?"

"She likes to express her opinions. She thought you kissing me in front of the kids was *'scandalous.'*" I held up my fingers, making air quotes.

He cupped my cheek, looking concerned. "I caused you trouble?"

I shook my head. "She causes herself the trouble. I don't care about her opinion. I think she was jealous you kissed me, not her. Besides—" I grinned "—I like your kind of trouble."

"I don't want to cause you problems at work. I wanted to show you I wasn't hiding. I would never hide my affection for you."

"I know. I love that about you. How open you are with Mia. Holly and the girls. Me. Eleanor went through a nasty divorce a few years ago, and she is still bitter. I ignore her the best I can."

"If she gives you any trouble, let me know. I'll talk to her."

"You don't have to fight my battles for me, Simon."

"If I caused them, I should."

"You caused nothing. It's her problem."

He leaned forward and kissed me. His lips were warm, his late-afternoon scruff rubbing on my skin as he tilted his head, kissing me deeper. I wrapped my arms around his neck, enjoying the feel of him pressed against me. We were at the edge of the parking lot, hidden from the road by the thick trees, the school around the corner. We kissed for long moments until he drew back, resting his forehead against mine.

"Now I'm the one with the problem," he muttered lowly.

I began to laugh, reaching down and stroking him through his jeans. "You have a big one there, don't you?"

"You're not helping, Chippy."

"You want to slip into the woods, and I'll solve your little problem?"

He looked down at me, shocked. "You're not serious."

I had only been teasing, but suddenly, the thought of him in my mouth, groaning his release as he gripped the bark of the tree turned me on. I knew his ex had been cold, only using sex as a weapon, disdaining any spontaneity. I wanted to give him this moment. To watch him dissolve under my touch. I slowly shook my head. "Not kidding."

His gaze darkened, and his grip on me tightened. "Amy," he ground out. "Don't tempt me."

I eased back, heading toward the trees. I glanced over my shoulder. "Come join me, Simon. You know you want to." I waggled my fingers. "Let's go, big boy."

He caught up to me fast, spinning me around. His kiss was blazing hot. He delved his hands under my sweater, spreading his fingers wide on my skin. I pushed him back against the thick trunk of an evergreen tree and dropped to my knees. I reached for his belt.

"Let's see what I can do to help you."

His head fell back, and he groaned as I engulfed him in my mouth.

I planned on making it good for him.

SIMON

I sat at the table, smiling at the antics of the girls. They were coloring, laughing, and enjoying themselves. Although Mia was older than her cousins, the girls got along well and were good friends. Evan had Brandon on his knee and was sipping a cup of coffee. Holly and Amy were talking quietly. Holly rolled her eyes when Amy told her about Eleanor. "She's an excellent by-the-book teacher. Never goes outside the lines, never bends." She paused. "Never smiles. She was one of the adults on a field trip, and she chastised Angela for laughing too much. Called her a troublemaker. I spoke with the principal about her and told her when Angela started grade three I would not allow her to be in that class. Evan wanted to go to the school and chat with her himself, but I convinced him to leave it. I think it might have gotten ugly. He wants the kids to be kids. Laugh, play, enjoy their childhood. Eleanor seems to want them to be little robots that are perfect." She finished her coffee. "She doesn't like me either, Amy, so you aren't alone."

"I'm glad Mia isn't in her class."

Holly hummed in agreement. "Mrs. Reynolds is lovely."

I listened to their conversation, not saying much.

Evan leaned over. "You okay, Simon? You seem distracted."

"I'm great. Just enjoying the evening."

The truth was, I was still reeling in shock over Amy and her boldness. Recalling every second of our fast tryst in the woods. The contrast of her hot mouth engulfing my cock and the cool air that surrounded us. How the bark of the tree bit into my skin as I gripped the trunk. The sound of my low groans building in my chest. The blistering heat of my orgasm as it snaked through me, and I came harder than I had ever come before in my life.

In a patch of woods. Next to my daughter's school. We could have been caught.

It was dangerous.

Exhilarating.

I had never felt so free. So safe to experience such desire. I had no idea such passion existed.

All because of the pretty, free spirit sitting across from me, teasing my daughter and fitting in with my new family so well.

I caught her eye, and she winked before returning her attention to Mia. Evan caught our silent exchange and grinned. "It's nice to see you so happy, Simon."

"It's nice to feel this way." I sat back, picking up my coffee. "I have a favor."

"Ask away."

"Would you and Holly keep Mia for a weekend?"

"That isn't a favor. You know we adore her." He helped Brandon choose a new crayon, holding them up until his son picked one. "You want to take Amy away for a weekend?"

"Yeah. And if it goes well, I want to take them both somewhere. There's a place back in Ontario that is a kid-friendly resort. I could combine a business and family trip. Give the girls a spa day together while I take care of some face-to-face business, then have the weekend."

"Sounds like fun."

"You should come. We can get a couple of suites. They have in-house babysitting too. We can enjoy the evenings. Go out for a couple of nice dinners. Niagara Falls is close."

He rubbed his bottom lip. "I'll talk to Holly."

"I know Ontario isn't your favorite place, but I doubt we'll run into anyone either of us knows there. And we aren't going anywhere fancy. Just a fun few days. The kids would love it. I bet Holly would enjoy the spa day."

He nodded. "They would. I could hang with my little man here and relax."

"This place has a ton of activities. Mia would love having you guys with us."

"Okay, I'll talk to Holly. In the meantime, plan your weekend with Amy."

I clapped him on the shoulder. "Great. Thanks."

On the way home, Mia chatted from the back seat. "Amy, can we have a picnic?"

Amy turned in her seat. "Like the one we had a

couple of weeks ago? When we sat by the water and walked on the dock?"

"Yes," Mia replied. "That was fun." She wrinkled her nose. "Except the funny red things."

"Lobster," Amy said with a chuckle. We had bought some lobster on the wharf to take home, and Mia had stared at them in wonder, unsure what to make of them. She was still not adventuresome in the food department. Fish and chips was the best I'd managed to convince her to try, and she had liked them. Amy got her to eat a bite of the lobster the next day, but she wasn't overly keen on them, which was fine. She would probably change her mind when she got older.

"Maybe instead of a picnic, we could eat at the café on the wharf," I offered. "You liked their fish and chips."

"And a whoopie pie?" Mia asked hopefully.

I chuckled. "If you eat your lunch, yes."

"Can we go on a boat?"

"We'll see."

My phone rang as we got to the house, and I frowned at the number, recognizing a client who only ever called when he needed help—and he had never called this late into the evening. "I need to take this."

Amy waved me off. "No problem. I'll get Little Miss ready for bed and read to her."

Grateful, I kissed her, then Mia, and headed for my office.

AMY

Mia giggled as I rinsed her hair. "That tickles."

I laughed with her. "Do you want me to braid your hair before you go to bed?"

"In the pretty pattern?"

"Yes."

"Oh, please!"

"Okay, out you get, Little Miss, and get in your jammies."

I let the water out of the tub and smiled as Mia padded down the hall. I loved these little moments with her. Simple, homey, routine things. Bath time. Braiding her hair. Listening to her natter about her day. It felt so domestic and natural. Knowing Simon would join us when he was done on his call made me happy. I tried to tell myself not to rush ahead, not to get used to it. We had only been dating and together for a few weeks, but I knew in my heart of hearts, I was already in love with Simon. With Mia. When I was at my apartment last night, I felt out of place. It was silent. No Simon talking or watching a TV program, his glasses perched on the bridge of his nose, giving him a serious air. No Mia asking questions, sneaking in another hug or begging for a cookie before she went to bed. I had felt lonely and displaced.

Here I felt needed. Wanted.

I shook my head and headed to Mia's room. I could hear the timbre of Simon's voice from downstairs, so I knew he was still busy. I sat on the floor, and Mia sat between my legs as I brushed her hair and began the intricate double French braiding. Simon was adept at braiding, which surprised me, but the double French one was too much. I enjoyed doing it with Mia. She loved the attention, and it was "our thing." We chatted a little, but I noticed she'd gone quieter than normal.

"Are you tired?" I asked. "First day of school and everything?"

"A little."

"Only four days this week," I said. "You can sleep in a little on Saturday, and then we'll do something fun."

"What if it rains?"

"We can still go out for lunch. Maybe have a movie afternoon."

"That sounds like fun."

"Good. I need an elastic, please."

Mia handed me one over her shoulder. "How come you don't have any kids, Amy?"

I laughed lightly. "I haven't found the right man to have kids with."

"Some of the kids in my class only have moms. How does that work?"

"Um, it's a bit complicated."

She sighed. "Dad says that a lot."

"He's right."

I switched to the other side, my fingers separating and braiding her hair. She spoke again.

"You'd be a good mom."

"You think so?"

She was silent for a moment. "The lady who was supposed to be my mom isn't a good one."

"Sometimes being a mom isn't for everyone," I said gently. "But you have an awesome daddy who loves you very much."

"I know. But sometimes I'd like a mom too." She became quiet, her voice dropping. "Sometimes I wonder why she couldn't love me. Maybe I was a bad baby."

"No," I said firmly. "You were a great baby. Your dad told me. Your mom—"

She cut me off. "I don't think of her as my mom. Just a lady who grew me in her tummy and gave me to Daddy."

I was surprised at the maturity of her thinking, but Simon was right. She was very smart and wise for her age a lot of the time. Other times, she was just Mia, the funny little girl I had come to adore.

I finished her hair and turned her to face me. "That's okay, Mia. You can think of her any way you want. They're your feelings, and you have every right to have them."

"Real moms are there. They love you. Protect you."

Before I could respond, she kept going. I heard a floorboard squeak, and I knew Simon had come upstairs and he could hear her as well. "That lady just gave me away to Daddy. She never comes to see me. Would you give me away, Amy?"

"No."

"Neither would Daddy. He protects me."

"He does."

"Auntie Holly is a real mom. She stayed with her kids. Last week, another girl was being mean to Hannah in the park, and before Uncle E could even move, Holly was there, telling the kid not to be so mean. She scolded her and made sure Hannah was okay. She hugged Hannah and kissed her knee where she'd fallen when the girl pushed her. Sometimes I wish I had a mom who did that too." She twisted around and looked at me, her pain in her eyes. "But I love my daddy. Is that okay?"

"Oh, Mia," I whispered. "Yes, it's okay to want a mom. I know you love your daddy. He knows it too. And he loves you so much."

"Could you be my mom?" she asked.

My heart stuttered at her question, and I knew I had to answer carefully.

"I don't know what the future holds. You and your dad have to decide that one day. But Mia, I promise you, no matter what happens, I'll always be your friend, okay?"

"You won't leave me like she did?"

"Your friend," I repeated. "Always. Even if your

dad finds you a new mom you love more than me. Because friends are forever."

"I would like it to be you."

"Sweetheart," I said softly, pushing a wisp of hair I'd missed off her face. "That is a grown-up decision. Sometimes when you're big, things aren't so easy. Your dad and mom separated so they could be happier on their own. Your daddy was happiest with you. He's going to give you the best mom one day. But it's a decision he is going to take a while to make. You can't rush him. He has to make it the right way, or he'll be unhappy again."

"If he wanted it to be you, would you say yes?"

I had no idea what brought on this serious conversation. The first day of school? The new kids and seeing all the moms pick them up? Something else? But I was unsure how to respond. Simon walked in, dropping to his knees in front of Mia. He stroked her cheek.

"Sweet Pea, you can't ask Amy that yet. Daddy and Amy have to get to know each other better. Amy's right, and it's a big decision. But once we make it, I'll talk to you about it, okay? Until then, it's just us. And I will never leave you," he assured her.

"I love you, Daddy," she whispered. "Even if I don't get a mommy, I still love you."

"And I love you." He bent and kissed her, pulling her into his arms. He met my eyes, and I had to blink and look away. He said so much without saying a word. He felt Mia's pain and her want for a mother.

He wanted to give that to her. He didn't know any more than I did what had brought this up today, but he wanted to comfort and reassure her. I stood, indicating I would go downstairs. He nodded, and I pressed a kiss to Mia's head, leaving them.

CHAPTER ELEVEN

SIMON

Mia fell asleep in my arms, and I tucked her in, staring down at her. For someone her age, she was remarkably mature. I wondered what had led to the conversation I'd overheard between her and Amy. She'd seemed in good spirits earlier.

Perhaps it was something she'd been thinking about more than I realized.

I headed down to see Amy, hoping she was still there. I was relieved to see her curled up on the sofa, and I dropped beside her, offering her a rueful smile.

"Sorry. I have no idea what brought on that conversation with Mia."

Amy smiled. "I wondered myself. Maybe seeing all the moms pick up their kids. Or maybe it's been on her mind awhile. She mentioned something about the park."

I nodded. "She told me about it. Evan called

Holly a fierce momma lion, and Mia thought that was cool. I guess a daddy lion isn't enough." I sighed.

Amy shook her head and cupped my cheek. "You are enough, Simon. She was just being wistful. I liked the fact that she felt comfortable enough to talk to me. Little girls sometimes just—" She shrugged "—need a mommy. I see it at school with divorced parents sometimes."

"She's never seemed to miss Kelsey before."

"She's growing up. Her needs change. But she's fine. She has you. Holly and Evan. She has an amazing support system around her."

"She likes you."

Amy smiled at me. "I like her. And you. But we're still pretty new, Simon. Neither of us wants to rush into anything."

I clasped our hands, staring down at our entwined fingers. I was silent for a moment, choosing my words carefully.

"After Kelsey, I never imagined having someone else in my life again. She hurt me terribly, and even worse, she turned her back on our child, which, regardless of her age, hurt her. I've tried to do my best for Mia. Moving here seemed right. She had Evan and Holly. Her cousins. I could be around more. But she is still missing something."

"She was just having a moment, Simon," Amy assured me. "She is. But she'll be fine."

I looked up, meeting her lovely eyes, the gentleness of her gaze soaking into me, warming me.

"I'm not rushing when I say I see a future with you, Amy. I see you in this house with us." I swallowed. "I see you with Mia. With a child we make together. I'm not getting any younger, and I want that soon. I want to be around for them as they're growing up."

"You-you want a child with me?"

I turned so I was facing her. "I want it all with you. The more time I spend with you, the more I want it. I don't want you to go home at night. I don't want to wake up in the morning without you beside me. I want to hear you laughing with Mia. See your jars and bottles on the bathroom vanity. Mutter about how much closet space you take. I want it all with you." I drew in a deep breath. "And I'm afraid you might not want it as much as I do. And that frightens me more than anything else."

She blinked, then looked down at our hands. She didn't say anything for a minute and I was afraid I'd said too much. Then a tear splashed on our joined hands, and I slid my fingers under her chin, lifting her face and meeting her watery gaze. "Too much?" I asked.

"Too beautiful. You really want all that with me, Simon? I'm not too much, too out there?"

"No," I said firmly. "I love your free spirit. I adore the way you seize life and live it. I think the way you dress is sexy and beautiful." I edged closer. "And your spontaneity. I really love that." Brushing a finger over her lips, I smiled. "I've never felt this way before, Amy. Ever. You make me happy. Aside from Mia, no one and nothing has ever made me feel the way you do. I don't want that to end."

"You make me happy too."

"And Mia?"

"I adore her, Simon." She paused. "I adore both of you."

I shifted closer. "That frightens you?"

"Some moments, yes. How much you mean to me so quickly. After what happened with my ex, I didn't want to put myself out there again, risk being hurt and rejected. I swore I would never try to change myself to conform to someone else's idea of what I should be. I almost did for him."

"I don't want you to change. I like you just the way you are." I pulled her onto my lap, unable to bear not touching her anymore. I tugged her close so our chests met and cupped her face. "I'm falling, Amy. I'm falling fast. I don't want to fight it. Don't ask me to." I brushed my mouth over hers. "Fall with me, please."

"I am," she whispered.

"Don't be scared, Chippy. I'm right there with you. I'll catch you."

Then my mouth was on hers. Claiming. Possessive. Needy.

We kissed endlessly, wrapped in each other's embrace. "Stay," I whispered against her mouth. "Please."

"Yes, but I have to leave early."

"I know. I'll take what I can get. For now."

I stood, flicking off the light and holding out my

hand. We walked upstairs, stopping by Mia's door. She was sprawled out, sound asleep, one leg stuck out of the blankets. "She's like you," I muttered. "No matter how often I tuck her in, the one leg is out."

Amy chuckled. "That will change once winter hits. It gets really cold here, and she'll want extra layers. You should get her a duvet. You can change the covers easily, so she can pick new ones, and they are light but warm."

"Good idea. We can go shopping on the weekend. We'll drive into Halifax, do some shopping, and have lunch. She'd love that as much as another picnic, or we can do that Sunday."

In my room, I pushed the door behind me, leaving it slightly ajar. I stared at Amy as she tugged her blouse over her head and pulled out her hair clip so her wild curls fell over her shoulders. "You are so beautiful."

I stepped closer, running my finger over her satin skin. I traced her collarbone, over her shoulder and down her arm, then back up to her neck. I smiled at the shiver that ran through her. I touched her bottom lip with my thumb, barely holding back my groan as she sucked it into her mouth, swirling her tongue around it.

"Such a talented, wicked mouth you have, Amy. Always smiling and sweet. But I know how naughty it can be. The things your tongue can do."

"Did you like earlier?" she asked.

"Did I like it?" I repeated, edging closer. "It was

all I could think about after. Your mouth around my cock with us hidden in the trees. Outside. I kept having to try to think of something else so my cock would stop attempting to tear through my pants."

She grinned and kissed the end of my thumb. "Good."

I popped the button on her skirt, tugging the zipper down and letting the material fall to the floor in a pile of lace and linen. "And now," I murmured, lifting her into my arms and depositing her on the bed. "I believe it is my turn."

She opened her arms and legs, letting me see her desire. I loved the fact that she was bare under her clothes and I was the only one who knew it. I also loved the fact that she wanted me as much as I wanted her.

"Lose the fabric, Simon," she murmured. "I want to feel you against me."

I grinned. "Yes, ma'am."

It was the only night she stayed until the weekend. We had dinner together one other night—I cooked, and she came over and spent the evening but left before Mia went to bed. I knew it was the start of the school year and she was still getting into her routine. Plus, she was taking some online courses she'd registered for before we'd started dating which would last for a few months. I understood, but I still hated it. The week after was a repeat of the one before. I would see her when I picked up Mia, we would talk, text, and call, but it wasn't the same. The house seemed empty without her, my bed too big, and the silence too loud once Mia went to bed. Mia missed her as well. How much I didn't realize until one night later the next week. We sat at the dinner table on Wednesday eating the spaghetti I had made, Mia noticeably quiet.

"Daddy," she asked suddenly. "We have lots of bedrooms, right?"

"Yes," I said. "We have four. I think that's plenty."

"We only use two."

"Yes." I frowned. "Why?"

"Couldn't you give one to Amy, and she could work here at night?"

I ruffled her hair. "You'd like that, would you?"

She nodded. "She could have supper with us and do her work. When she was finished, she could tuck me in."

"You don't like me tucking you in anymore, Sweet Pea?"

She made a "duh" face at me. "Of course, Daddy. But I like Amy. She smells good, and she rubs my head nicely." Her voice dropped to a whisper. "Like a mom."

My heart clenched at her words. I had talked to Holly about this, and she had confided that Mia was longing for a mom. And not just any mom. She wanted Amy. She adored her. I had to choose my words carefully.

"Mia, Amy is really busy with work and the courses she is taking. We can't put more demands on her time than she can spare. I don't want to cause her stress."

"What is that?"

"Like when you worry about something too much. Remember when you were worried about meeting Uncle E? Afraid he wouldn't like you, and it made you upset?"

She nodded. "But he loved me. So maybe Amy would love it if we made her a room."

"How about we talk to her about it when she comes over Saturday? She is going to spend the whole weekend with us."

She brightened noticeably. "Okay. But Daddy, she loves surprises."

I smiled and pushed her spaghetti closer. "Eat your supper, Sweet Pea."

Later when I tucked her in, I walked past the one bedroom that was completely empty. I stopped and flicked on the light, looking around. It was the smallest of the bedrooms but had, I thought, one of the best views, overlooking the water. It was painted in a soft cream, contrasting with the wood nicely. I rubbed my chin as an idea formed. A desk under the window, some bookshelves to hold supplies, and a comfortable chair would be easy to acquire. Maybe a throw rug. With the light and view during the day, and the quiet in the evening, it would be a good place to work.

Mia's insistence that Amy loved surprises kept running through my mind. I slid my cell phone from my pocket and called Holly, who answered on the first ring.

"Simon? Is everything okay?" she asked.

I chuckled. "Yes. But I need your help."

"Anything," she assured me.

"Could you come over tomorrow morning once the kids go to school?"

"I'll be there."

"Awesome."

The next morning, Holly arrived with Evan and Brandon in tow. I shook his hand, lifted Brandon up, grinning as he squealed in delight. "You get bigger every time I see you."

Holly laughed. "He grows in his sleep."

Evan took him, looking curious. "Holly says you need some help. What can we do?"

I felt a wave of gratitude flow over me. How I was lucky enough to have this family in my life, I didn't know. But they were kind and generous. So different from the rest of his clan. My own parents were deceased, and I was an only child. It was nice to be part of this family—to feel as if I belonged somewhere.

"I want to do something upstairs, but I need Holly's advice."

"Show us," she said.

I took them upstairs and showed them the room. "Mia and I miss Amy. I know she's busy with her courses and work. Mia had the idea of making her an office here so she could be with us more." I scratched the back of my neck. "Would she hate that?"

For a moment, Holly was quiet. She looked at me, laying her hand on my arm. "She would be thrilled if you made her a room. I saw her last night when I dropped off some supplies she wanted for a craft. Her apartment is small, and her desk is her dining room table. And she misses you guys as well. She wishes she hadn't signed up for this course."

"You think she'd use the room?"

"Yes." She turned to Evan. "What about that desk and bookshelf you finished a couple of weeks ago that you were going to sell online? They aren't too big, so they would be perfect here."

He nodded. "You're right."

"We can add a throw rug. A good chair—she mentioned her back hurt from sitting at the table on a hard chair all the time." Holly pointed around the room. "Desk there, bookshelf over there. Maybe a comfy chair in the corner. A good lamp."

"What about things for the walls? I know Amy likes to hang, ah, stuff," I asked.

"Oh," she said. "I can get a few of her photos from her Facebook page and print them. Then tell her to add whatever she wants. She would love that." She clasped her hands. "Simon, this is a wonderful idea."

135

"Yeah?"

"Yes," she enthused. "Evan can bring the desk and shelf over. I'll find a rug, chair, and lamp. You order a desk chair."

"What about curtains or other things?"

"Let Amy decide. I doubt she'll want to block the view."

"Can we get it done by Saturday?"

She grinned. "I'll have it done tomorrow. I saw a chair the other day at Wilson's antique store. Overstuffed, big, comfy. Recently reupholstered. I had nowhere to put it, but it would be perfect here." She looked giddy and threw her arms around me. "Amy will be so excited. No one has ever done anything so thoughtful for her. Her ex—" She stopped and shook her head. "I disliked him. He wasn't good enough for her."

"And I am?"

"You are perfect. You and Mia are exactly what she needs. She glows when she talks about you. And I know how much this will mean to her."

I drew in a deep breath. "It won't be too much? I don't want to push her, but I miss her. Mia misses her. She thought if Amy had a place she could work here, just knowing she was close would be a good thing."

"It's not too much. It's a lovely gesture."

She reached for her phone. "I'm calling Mr. Wilson to make sure that chair is still there. Then I need a cup of coffee and your laptop."

I grinned. "On it."

Friday afternoon, I picked up Mia and waited patiently until Amy was done with her students. I didn't hesitate as the last one left with their mother to walk over, and I bent to kiss Amy's cheek.

"Hello, Chippy."

She smiled at me, but I saw how tired she looked.

"Everything okay?"

"Yes. Long week."

Mia ran over to one of her classmates, talking excitedly to her. I smiled indulgently, thrilled how quickly she had found friends and settled here.

I met Amy's eyes, keeping my voice low. "Any chance I can convince you to come tonight for the weekend instead of the morning?"

Her smile was bright. "Really?"

I kissed the end of her nose in affection. "Really."

"Would I look too eager if I told you I already packed a bag in case?" she asked, looking worried.

"Would I look too eager if I threw you over my shoulder and carried you to the car?" I replied ardently.

"Um, maybe."

"Fine." I kissed her sweet mouth, not caring if we were being watched. "Get your stuff from the classroom and follow us home. Mia will be so excited."

"And her daddy?"

I kissed her again. "He'll show you how excited as

soon as Mia is asleep. Probably twice. Maybe three times," I mumbled against her lips.

"I look forward to it."

Mia rushed back over, waving a colorful piece of paper. "Daddy, I got invited to a birthday party next weekend. It's a sleepover."

I took the invitation, looking at it. I knew the girl and had met her parents. They had another daughter Angela's age, and they knew Holly and Evan. The mother, Trudy, came over with a smile. "Angela is coming as well. That way, Cindy has a playmate at the party."

I felt better knowing Angela would be there. Mia had never spent the night away at someone else's house besides Evan's, so this was new territory for both of us.

"We're doing a movie and pizza night," Trudy went on to explain. "The girls will 'camp out' on the family room floor. There'll be cake and presents and probably little sleep for anyone."

I laughed with her, knowing she was probably right.

"Holly is going to come help if that makes you feel better. And there are only six girls."

"Oh, great." I looked at Mia. "You want to do a sleepover with your friends, Sweet Pea?"

She nodded enthusiastically. "Yes!"

"Okay then, thanks. I'll call you this week."

Trudy smiled and waved, and I tucked the invite

into Mia's knapsack. Amy smiled, rubbing my arm. "They're a nice family."

"I know. I met them at a few of Holly and Evan's barbecues." I grinned at her. "Now, go get your stuff. We're going to pick up some Chinese food. Mia's been begging for egg rolls for days." I kissed her cheek. "We'll meet you at the house."

"Okay."

CHAPTER TWELVE

SIMON

Mia could hardly sit still during dinner. Even her favorite egg rolls couldn't keep her attention. Amy laughed at her, wiping her chin after the plum sauce dripped from her mouth while talking.

"What is going on with you, Sweet Pea?" she asked. "You're so excited."

Mia stopped, blinking. "You called me Sweet Pea. Only Daddy has ever called me that."

Amy grimaced. "Sorry. I hear your daddy say it all the time, and I guess it stuck and slipped out."

Mia shook her head. "No, I like it. You and Daddy can call me that. Like a special name."

"It is special, because you are special," Amy assured her, tapping her nose.

Mia grinned and finished her egg roll. I pushed away my plate, full from the noodles and honey garlic chicken I'd polished off along with my own egg rolls and wontons. Amy finished hers, reaching for her napkin to wipe her mouth. The kitchen was tidied fast, the leftovers put in the refrigerator, and the dishes loaded into the dishwasher.

"What shall we do tonight?" Amy asked.

"We have a surprise for you!" Mia burst out, unable to hold it in any longer.

I began to laugh, shocked she'd stayed silent this long. I had figured we wouldn't make it through dinner before she succumbed to her excitement.

"A surprise?" Amy repeated. "Did you pick up a cake?"

Mia shook her head. "It's better."

Amy widened her eyes. "Better than cake? I can't even imagine."

"It is!"

"Now I can't wait," Amy said, looking around, expecting to see some sort of treat in the kitchen.

I stood, extending my hand. "Come with me."

Amy stood, confused. Mia took her other hand, practically dragging her up the stairs. Amy looked even more confused as we stopped outside the closed door.

"Mia had an idea the other day that I thought was a good one."

"Okay?" she replied.

"No pressure, but if you want to use it, it's yours."

"Mine?" she questioned, now completely baffled.

I opened the door, and she stepped in, gasping.

Holly had done an amazing job. The corner held

a chair I could only describe as girly. Flowers, stripes, and ruffles. Deep and comfortable, with an ottoman to match, yet not too big. Perfect for Amy. She could sit and look at the view. The lamp behind it provided good light for her to see in the evenings. The desk and bookshelf I'd purchased from Evan were finished with a light stain, the wood grain showing through and fitting well in the space. He had refused payment, but I'd insisted—although I was certain the price he quoted was far less than he would have gotten elsewhere. I would make it up to him with the trip I was planning.

Holly had hung two pictures. One Amy had taken of the three of us on the beach one day, all smiling, with Mia squished between us, her expression one of pure delight. The other was one of Amy's photos from a small town on the island she loved to visit. I wanted to take her there for a weekend soon. A few books had been placed on the shelves, and a pretty container held some pens on the desk. A few other items had been scattered around that Holly thought were needed. My query as to the need for baskets was only met with a shake of her head. I stopped asking, realizing it was best to leave it to her judgment. She knew Amy well.

The rug Holly found had more flowers in the same pink, green, and cream shades as the comfy, feminine chair. I'd made sure the desk chair had proper support and a back rest so Amy didn't tire her muscles as she worked. Holly had softened it with a blanket draped over the back. Aside from my giving Holly carte blanche on the room, and paying for things, the chair was my only contribution, along with a fresh bouquet of flowers on the desk I had picked up. Wild flowers I knew Amy would love. The room was simple, pretty, and useful. Ready for Amy to add items as she wanted and needed.

If she wanted the room.

She covered her mouth as she took it all in. Touched the chair. Ran her finger over the smooth wood top of the desk. Looked at the photos. Scrunched her toes on the thick rug. Admired the flowers. Then slowly, she turned to Mia and me. Mia grasped my hand, as anxious as I was for her reaction.

"How?"

"Holly helped."

Her blue eyes were bright with tears. "This is for me?"

"So you can come here and work," Mia said. "I won't bother you, but I'd like knowing you are here. I miss you sometimes."

Amy's eyes became brighter, the tears beginning to overflow.

"No pressure, Chippy," I said softly. "But we both miss having you around. Your apartment is too small for an office, and we have lots of space. If you want it."

"If I want it?" she repeated, sounding incredulous. "This is the most wonderful thing anyone has ever done for me." She dropped to her knees, holding out her arms. Mia broke from me, lunging into her embrace. There were tears from both of them and the words "I love you" murmured and declared.

I dropped to the floor beside them. "Can I join in the lovefest?"

I was ensconced in arms, covered with kisses, both tiny little pecks from Mia and far more passionate ones from Amy. She wrapped her arms around my neck, whispering her praise, sobbing her thanks, and murmuring the words I had longed to hear. "I love you, Simon."

I wrapped her close. "I love you, Amy."

"I love you too!" Mia crowed.

I laughed as we snuggled, a big ball of happiness. I felt a moment of pure, unadulterated love. It was a moment I basked in.

And one I wanted many more of.

We tried out the chair, all three of us fitting in it. Amy curled into my side, Mia on my lap. Mia pointed out everything, making sure Amy missed nothing.

"That's the picture we took when we ate lobster!" she exclaimed.

"Well, Amy and I ate lobster," I reminded Mia.

"I'll eat more next time."

"Okay." I pressed a kiss to her head.

"I helped Holly pick the rug. I made sure it was soft and warm. And the blanket."

"It's all perfect," Amy assured her.

"Will you use it?" Mia asked.

"Yes."

The next while was filled with more talking, sharing, and laughing. Then Mia grew quiet, and after a while, Amy whispered, "She's asleep."

"I'm not surprised," I whispered back. "She was so excited last night, it took forever to get her to sleep. She was up early, making sure the room was just right."

Amy cupped my cheek, moving her fingers in restless circles. "It is. It's a wonderful surprise. I meant what I said earlier. No one has ever done something so amazing for me."

"You can bring whatever you want and make it your own space. I just asked Holly to help set up the basics."

"It's already beautiful. And so thoughtful."

"It's selfish. I miss you too much."

She tilted her head, then leaned forward and kissed me. "Why don't you tuck our girl in and meet me in our room? I want to be selfish too."

The use of the word "our" did something to me. It unfurled a tightness in my chest I'd been carrying for a long time.

"Meet you there."

AMY

I rested against the padded headboard, looking around Simon's room. It was spacious, with a walk-in closet and a large master bath. His king-sized bed was a dream to sleep on. I couldn't imagine him fitting on my double bed. He'd have to lie at an angle, and even then, his feet would hang out.

I heard his footsteps, and I straightened my shoulders and arranged myself in what I hoped was a seductive pose. I had bought a sexy nightgown—if you wanted to call the wisp of lace and fabric a nightgown. It was sheer and barely reached my thighs. The lace appliqués only highlighted my nipples instead of offering any modesty. But it was pretty, and I had a feeling Simon would enjoy taking it off.

He came in, shutting the door behind him. He was silent for a moment, appraising me. His gaze took in the diaphanous fabric, or the lack of it, really. A smile played on his lips as he strolled toward the bed, pulling his shirt over his head and crawling up the mattress toward me. The predatory gleam in his eyes made me shiver. He grasped my legs, stroking over the calves, then tugged my knees apart and fitted himself between them.

"I'm not the only one with a surprise tonight," he muttered, tracing one long finger over the thin strap, then following the lace down and stroking my hardening nipple. "Shame, though."

I met his eyes. "Shame? You don't like it?"

"I love it. But it's not going to last." Then he was on me, his mouth hard on mine. His kiss was explosive. Possessive. Commanding. He kissed me as if he needed my mouth to survive. God knew it felt as if I needed his. I gripped his biceps, anchoring myself to him as he ravished my mouth. Licking, sucking, biting, his low groans and hot breath making me lose control. The thin fabric tore under his fingers as he split it down the back, ripping it from my body so our chests melded together. I slid my hands under his waistband, yanking his sweats down, the two of us managing to get them off without our mouths separating. His rougher skin rubbed against mine, his cock hot and heavy between us. I wrapped my hand around him, swirling my thumb on the tip as he groaned. He pulled his mouth from mine, kissing me everywhere. My neck, shoulders, ears, across my collarbone. He sucked my nipple into his mouth, his tongue playing with it until the hard peak was glistening and aching. He did the same with the other one as I caressed him, one hand on his dick while I stroked his balls, rubbed my feet along his legs, cupped his firm ass and begged him for more.

More of his mouth. His touch. His teeth.

And his cock. I needed it inside me. Filling me. Claiming me.

He sat back, his hair a mess from my hands, his lips swollen and wet.

"You want my cock, Amy? You want me inside you?"

"Yes," I begged. "Take me, Simon. Make me yours."

"Are you?" he challenged. "Are you mine?"

I knew what he wanted. What he needed. The words that were so important to him.

"Yes, I'm yours." I met his intense gaze. "I love you."

He gripped my legs and pulled me up his thighs, burying himself inside me. It was hard, deep, and perfect. He held my hips, thrusting into me, hitting my clit as he moved. I was awash in sensations, filled and wrapped in him, but it wasn't enough. I needed more. I needed closer. I reached for him, and he knew. He slid his arms under me, pulling me to his chest, sinking even deeper inside me. I wrapped my legs around his hips and we moved, the rise and fall of our bodies in perfect sync. He lowered his head, capturing my mouth, and I was surrounded by him. Our skin rubbed with a delicious friction, our chests pressed tightly together. He held me in an iron grip, his mouth moving with mine, his tongue imitating his hips, thrusting, seeking, giving. I grasped at his shoulders, gripped his hair, stroked his wide back. I couldn't get close enough. Feel him enough.

And then my body locked down, my orgasm washing over me like a wave. Long, powerful, and consuming. I cried out my release into his mouth as he stiffened, his arms holding me so tightly I could barely breathe, a deep, muffled groan sounding in his chest as he succumbed to the pleasure. His mouth gentled, becoming softer. Sweeter. He kissed my cheeks, my eyes, then buried his face into my neck, still rocking, both of us basking in the afterglow, satisfaction and warmth making us content. Lowering us to the mattress, he lay beside me and cupped the back of my head, looking down at me. I opened my eyes and met his gaze.

"Amy," he whispered.

I traced his mouth, still damp from our passion. "Hi."

He smiled. "I love you."

I snuggled into his chest, letting his love saturate my body and his words fill my heart.

"I'm never letting you go," he vowed. "You complete me in a way I didn't know existed. Promise me you'll stay with me. With us. Build a life with me." His arms tightened. "Let me be yours."

I tilted up my head. "You want to be mine? You want everyone to know that?"

"Yes. I want everyone to know I belong to you. That you're mine. I love you, Amy. Every single part of you. The flower child, the free spirit, the loving woman, the teacher, the artist, the sexy wanton in my bed. The thinker. The mother in you. All of it." He pressed a kiss to my mouth. "I love all of you."

I felt the tears build in my eyes, and he kept talking. "So does Mia. She adores you. I have never seen her get this attached to someone. She loves Holly, but she needs you. You give her something I can't—that no one else can. You give me something I didn't know I needed. I don't even know what it is, except it's all you. We both need you."

"And I'm enough," I said in wonder.

"I don't want to change anything about you. You fit with us so well. You bring a light and warmth into our lives I never realized was missing. You are more than enough." He paused. "Are you willing to take us on?"

I stared into his hopeful, anxious gaze. I traced my finger over his jaw and smiled. "Yes, Simon Fletcher, I'm willing to take you on. I love you both, and I want my future to have you both in it."

His smile was wide and his kiss passionate. "We'll take it as slow or fast as you want," he promised. "Don't stay away from us because you think you should, or society thinks we're going too fast. I don't care what anyone thinks but us. As long as I know we're headed for the same goal, I'm good. Just promise me I can see you more. Work here a couple nights—or every night, if you want. We'll figure it all out. Together."

Together—what a lovely word.

I wrapped my arms around his neck, and he held me close.

"Yes."

CHAPTER THIRTEEN

AMY

The next morning, I woke to the smell of coffee and the sound of giggles coming from the kitchen. I could hear the deep timbre of Simon's voice hushing Mia, then his low laughter as she no doubt did something cute that amused him. I loved their relationship. His utter adoration of her and the way she hero-worshiped him. I pulled myself up into a sitting position, resting against the fluffy pillows and drawing my legs up to my chest. I looked around the room, the morning sun spilling through the windows and the view of the water. It danced and swirled in the breeze, a multitude of colors captured in the sunshine. It would be a great day for a picnic.

I thought about last night. The surprise Simon and Mia had for me. The beautiful office I could work from so I would be close to them.

Because they liked having me here and missed me when I wasn't around.

It was still a foreign feeling to me—being so accepted. So wanted.

And the office was simply perfect.

I had hated going back to my apartment at the end of the day last week. My highlight had been the brief glimpses of Simon when he picked up Mia. Our phone calls and texts. The dinner we had shared. My place seemed so cramped and lonely now. My bed was empty and cold. I missed Simon's warmth, his arms around me, his breath on my neck as he would pull me to his chest and hold me close. Dinner was lonely and quiet without Mia's giggles and questions.

The truth was, I liked being here with them. Feeling as if I belonged. As if I mattered. My ex had shattered my self-confidence to the point I was skeptical I would be able to trust anyone again, yet with Simon, my trust was absolute. After the rocky start and his complete honesty, he gave me no reason to doubt him. He was clear and open with his feelings and affection. I liked how he made me feel. Wanted. Adored. Needed. Loved.

And suddenly, I wanted to be close to him.

Throwing back the covers, I slipped from the bed and pulled on one of Simon's T-shirts and a pair of leggings I had left there. I headed downstairs, walking into the kitchen and smiling at the sight. Simon by the stove, helping Mia pour the pancake batter into the pan, gently coaching her.

"Not too much, Sweet Pea, or we won't get many in the pan."

"Like that, Daddy?"

He kissed her head. "Perfect."

Then he caught sight of me, and a wide smile broke out on his face. "Look who's awake."

Mia turned her head, smiling and looking so much like Simon it made me grin. "Amy!" she exclaimed, clambering off the stool and rushing my way. "Daddy and I are making pancakes," she said, throwing herself into my arms. "I was gonna come wake you up."

"Well, I smelled the deliciousness coming from the kitchen, and I couldn't stay in bed any longer." I straightened, still holding Mia to my side.

Simon handed me a mug of coffee, bending over and kissing me. "Good morning, Chippy."

"Hi." I smiled against his mouth.

He kissed me again. "Hi."

"You guys kiss a lot. More than a dating kiss. Is that 'cause you're in love?" Mia asked, rubbing the end of her nose.

Simon grinned, ruffling Mia's hair. "Yeah, kiddo. Something like that."

"I am not kissing boys."

"Good!" we both exclaimed.

Laughing, she ran from the room. "I'm gonna get dressed!"

I sipped my coffee as Simon returned to the pancakes.

"Your phone has buzzed a few times," he said, indicating the counter. "I plugged it in for you."

"Oh." I grabbed it and groaned as I read the messages waiting.

"Problem?" he asked.

"No, it's my mom, reminding me I promised to go into Halifax tomorrow and have lunch. My brother, Sheldon, will be there as well. He's home for a visit."

Simon looked disappointed but shrugged. "Well, we'll have to make the best of today, then."

I hesitated, then wrapped my hands around my mug. "Would you like to come with me?"

He paused. "With you?"

"You and Mia. Come with me for lunch." I swallowed. "Meet my family."

He carried over a plate of pancakes, setting them on the table. He sat beside me, taking my hand. "Are you ready for that, Amy? To introduce Mia and me to your parents?"

I didn't hesitate. "Yes."

He broke into a smile. "Then I would love to meet them. We'll do a picnic around here today and head into Halifax tomorrow."

"Okay. We can stop at the bedding store to pick out a duvet for Mia before we go to my parents'. I'll call my mom after breakfast."

"She won't mind?"

I laughed. "She will go insane. More people to cook for and a little girl to fawn over? It'll make her day."

He pulled me close. "And meeting her future son-in-law? She'll like that too, right?"

My heart rate picked up hearing him say those words. To believe in our future that strongly.

"I might not use those exact words when introducing you," I said carefully.

"Did they like your ex?"

"No. They didn't like how he treated me."

"Then they are gonna love me. I plan on treating you like a queen. My queen."

"You already do."

He leaned forward and kissed my neck, sending a delicious shiver down my spine. "I'm only getting started, Amy." He trailed his lips up to my ear, teasing the sensitive area behind the lobe. "And if my daughter weren't about to appear and demand pancakes and your attention, I would show you how incredibly sexy you are in my shirt. But I'll take a rain check for later." He covered my mouth with his, kissing me hard.

Mia appeared, skidding to a halt by the table, her deep sigh of annoyance separating us. "You're still kissing? That's even more than Uncle E and Auntie Holly. I thought they kissed a lot." She shook her head. "Why?"

"More dating rules," Simon said, standing with a droll wink. "I have to kiss Amy lots so she likes me. The more I kiss her, the more she stays with us."

"Oh," she said, her eyes wide. "Okay, then. You can kiss her."

Simon nodded sagely. "Good plan."

To say my mom was excited when I called her to tell her I was bringing not only a man but his sweet little daughter with me for lunch would be an understatement.

"Daughter?" she asked. "How old?"

"Eight."

"Amy, is this serious?"

I looked out the window, watching Simon and Mia play tag on the front lawn. He was endlessly patient with her, and he had no problem being a fun, silly dad. I was never able to stress to parents enough the importance of playing with their kids—the bonding, the memories they would create. It was important. Simon got that. He loved spending time with Mia.

"Yeah, Mom, it is."

"You never mentioned him when you were home last visit."

I smiled ruefully. "It kinda happened fast. I met him a few times at social gatherings, then suddenly, we were a thing."

"Does he treat you well?"

I knew my parents had disliked Darren. They didn't like how he spoke to me or how he picked me apart all the time. The way he made me feel I wasn't enough. When we'd broken up, they had been pleased, assuring me I could do better.

And they had been right.

"Oh, Mom. Like I'm the most important woman in the world." I told her about the office. Our picnics. How much I enjoyed spending time with Mia.

"It sounds as if you're in very deep."

I sighed. "I think I am."

"Then we look forward to seeing them tomorrow."

I hung up and went downstairs. We'd packed some snacks and water. A couple of sandwiches in case Mia got hungry. Crustless rolled PB & J—her favorite now, too.

Simon walked in, windblown and smiling. He pressed a kiss to my head. "All okay for tomorrow?"

"Yes. They are looking forward to meeting you."

"What can I bring? Wine? Something stronger for your dad? We should get some flowers for your mom."

I patted his chest. "Maybe a bottle of wine. My dad likes beer and not much else. Flowers would be nice but not necessary."

"I disagree. I need to wow them—get them on my side so I have backup. Flowers, wine, beer—all of it."

I laughed at his silliness. "Okay, Simon. Whatever you say."

"There is a game like that."

"Oh really?"

"Yes—where you have to do everything Simon says."

"Is that a fact?" I asked, crossing my arms.

"Yes. Like Simon says, Amy kiss me. You have to."

"I didn't agree to play."

"Well then, Simon says Simon kiss Amy." He pulled me into his arms and did just that. Then he whispered, "Simon says Amy spend the whole weekend. Simon says Amy be naked later and in his bed. Simon says Amy will come four times before midnight. Twice after."

"Simon is very demanding."

"But Simon likes this game."

I began to laugh, and he pressed a kiss to my head. "Simon also likes you."

I looked up at him. "I love Simon," I whispered.

He smiled. "Simon says you have to say that every day."

"Okay."

"Now Simon says it's picnic time or a little girl I know is going to come in here and wonder why we're kissing—again."

"Then off we go."

He bent and kissed me one more time. "Simon says he is keeping Amy." Then he held out his hand. "Let's go."

I rather liked this game.

We pulled up to my parents' house, and I was hit with a case of nerves. I looked over at Simon, who seemed calm. "We don't have to do this."

He unbuckled his seat belt. "Of course we do. I want to meet your parents and your brother. Let them get to know us. He touched my cheek, stroking the skin gently. "It's all going to be good, Chippy."

"My dad can be outspoken. So can my brother. He's older and protective. And my mom is really affectionate—"

He cut me off with a laugh. "Thanks for the heads-up. You forget I have the ultimate weapon."

"Which is?"

He indicated the back seat. "The sweetest kid on the planet. No one can resist her. Trust me. She'll have them eating out of the palm of her hand in two minutes flat. They'll love her, and I'm in. All's good." He slid from the car. "Come on, Amy. Let's do this."

I undid my seat belt and got out of the car. Simon helped Mia out, and I handed her the flowers she had picked out for my mom. Simon had a six-pack of my dad's favorite beer, and I had two bottles of wine—a white for my mother and a red for my brother, Sheldon.

"We have a lot of liquor here," I observed.

Simon chuckled. "Soon-to-be in-laws are more open to the idea of me if soused," he deadpanned.

I slapped his arm. "Stop it. Be serious."

Laughing, he took Mia's hand, and she slipped her other one into mine. "I am."

Simon laughed loudly, slapping his knee. "Of course she did. What else would you expect?"

My dad shook his head, grinning. "Every damn cage. All the mice were running around the classroom. Frogs hopping on every surface. Amy yelling for them all to run and be free."

"Or hop," Sheldon added, chuckling.

I shook my head. "I was eight. Every time I walked past the science room and saw the cages, it upset me. I decided to do something about it." I defended myself, even though I was laughing as well. I recalled the chaos and my parents showing up at school. As well as the stern lecture I received in front of the principal, even though their reaction behind closed doors was far less firm. My parents knew how I felt about animals and understood. But we agreed I would avoid the science room the bigger kids used and instead concentrate on schoolwork. My mom and I started volunteering at the animal shelter, and that helped me. I still did when I had time. I wondered how Simon would feel about me taking Mia to help one day. I would have to ask him.

The afternoon couldn't be going better. Simon was right, and they fell for Mia right away. She handed Mom the flowers, informed her she was hungry and she liked cookies, and that was that. Told her all about the pretty duvet covers we'd picked out and how much she loved to snuggle under blankets.

She giggled at my dad and fell in love with Sheldon when he took her outside, pushing her on the tire swing we'd had in the backyard for years. Simon and my dad had a beer and bonded. He ate two helpings of my mom's roast beef and polished off a huge slice of dessert, declaring her apple-cranberry the best pie he had ever tasted. He chatted with my brother about his work on a cruise ship.

"You must see a lot of great ports."

Sheldon nodded. "I do, but it's a lot of work. I'm one of the head stewards, and I never know what I'm going to get asked for or to do from minute to minute. It's nice to be home and on a break for a while."

"You must miss being home at times. Is it a lifetime career?" Simon asked.

"I hadn't planned it to be, but the years have just flown by. But I love to travel. To explore new places. I take different contracts, so I can see different places. Some are four months, others are ten. Some I enjoy so much I sign on for a second term, but I usually move every year. I love being on the water. I don't plan on doing this forever, but right now, it's great. Room and board are part of the package, so I bank my paychecks, or at least most of them. I stay here or with friends out west when I'm off. No point in paying rent when I am never there. A bit nomadic, but I love it—at least for now. I figure another four years or so, then I'll settle and figure out what I want with the rest of my life." He grinned. "Maybe find a woman who wants to take me on. One who loves to travel and I can show her all the places I love and discover some new ones together."

Mom interrupted him. "We love it when he comes home for a visit. Which isn't often enough. And with Amy busy with teaching, it's just us again."

Dad laughed. "Between your gardening, quilting, volunteering, and bridge games, you're rarely home either. I'm the one here, all alone." He made a sad face. "No one else around."

Mia climbed onto his lap. "You can come see me, or I can visit. Daddy can drop me off. You don't have to be alone."

My dad melted. Completely. My mom got tears in her eyes. I glanced at Simon, who winked.

"Told ya," he mouthed.

I got up to take my plate to the dishwasher so I didn't laugh.

He did, indeed.

It was almost dinnertime when we left. We hadn't been out of the driveway for ten minutes and Mia was out like a light in the back.

"They wore her out," Simon observed.

I laughed. "She wore them out. I bet they're already napping too."

He smirked, checking over his shoulder and changing lanes. "How old is your brother?"

"Thirty-nine."

"Married to the sea," he mused.

"He told me he's never found anyone he was remotely interested in enough to try to stay in one place for. I think he is a bit of a Casanova on the cruises." She frowned. "I hope he finds someone. He is a great guy."

"Yeah, I liked him."

I smiled and ran my finger down his cheek. "He liked you too."

"Your parents were high school sweethearts?"

"Yes."

"So long relationships run in your family. Marriage, ocean commitments, that sort of thing."

I rolled my eyes. "Whatever."

"Your parents are on board. Told you I had the ace. They loved her." He chuckled. "They insisted she call them Gramps and Gran."

"They liked both of you."

"Good. I liked them. It bodes well for the future."

I sighed. "Mom asked when the wedding was. She's as bad as you."

He peeked at me, then put his attention back on the road. "I heard her, and I told her I thought spring was doable when we were alone in the kitchen."

"Simon!"

He grinned. "No later than summer."

"We haven't discussed that. You are jumping ahead again."

He shook his head. "No. You're it for me, Amy. I already know that. I want to spend my life with you, and I want that life to start sooner rather than later. I'd marry you next week if I could."

I gaped at him. "Simon, you seriously need to slow your roll. I recall you telling me we'd take it at whatever speed I needed."

"Then you told me you loved me. That changed everything." He lifted my hand and kissed it. "I'm not pressuring you, Amy. I'm only saying what I'm thinking. I see us together. Raising a family, growing old. Enjoying life together. I'm not a kid anymore. I know what I feel, how you make me feel. I'm not going to change my mind. My feelings for you are only going to deepen. So why wait? Why not grab the moment and live it?"

"Shouldn't you be more, ah, reluctant, given your first experience?"

"No, I can't compare the two situations. With Kelsey, I was in a place in my life where I did things I thought I should. My friends were getting married. Having kids. She seemed to be perfect. I regretted it quickly, and it was only the news of—" He nodded toward the back seat "—that made me stay. But I knew it was a mistake and it wasn't going to last. But with you, it feels so right."

I huffed out a long breath. "One heck of a conversation for the drive home."

He chuckled. "Okay, let's change the subject. Will you go away with me next weekend?"

"Next weekend? But Mia has her sleepover," I protested.

"I love the fact that your first thought is about Mia. But Holly is going to be there to help. She thought it would be good for Mia to have her there so she was more comfortable. And if Mia isn't happy, Holly will take her and Angela home and keep her until we get back—we're only going to be an hour away. I just want some time alone with you."

"Where are we going?"

"Edgewater."

"I love it there!"

"I know. I want to go with you."

When I hesitated, he shook his head. "I have another trip planned to a place in Ontario for over the Thanksgiving weekend. Our family, plus Evan and his. Mia will love it. So she isn't being slighted in any way."

"You are amazing," I breathed out.

"I can arrange the honeymoon too."

I began to laugh. "How about we start with the weekend? You may change your mind. I do like to hog the bed."

"And you snore. Part of your charm." He linked our hands. "So, yes to the weekend with me?"

"Yes."

"Then I'll book it."

"Okay."

CHAPTER FOURTEEN

SIMON

The next week was far more enjoyable. Amy came over three nights, using her office, but being around at bedtime and after. Mia and I loved having her there, and she admitted she liked being with us far more than at her apartment.

"When is your lease up?" I asked.

"July next year."

"We need to look into sublets."

"Simon—" she began, but I cut her off.

"Or I can pay your rent. Not an issue."

She shook her head. "No, you cannot. That is not up for discussion."

"I can afford it."

"I assume you could if you made the offer, but once we decide on our future, I will figure out the apartment."

I stopped arguing, knowing I was going to have to

be crafty to come up with a solution. I changed the subject. "You ready for our weekend away?"

"Yes." She smiled and curled up in the corner of the sofa. "I'm looking forward to it."

"I reserved one of the cottages and booked dinner Friday night at that restaurant you said was good. We can decide about Saturday once we get there."

She ran a hand through her hair, the wild curls springing back into place. "That sounds wonderful."

I studied her. "You look tired, Chippy. I'm being selfish, aren't I? Keeping you up late, wanting you around all the time." I ran a finger down her cheek. "I should apologize and not do it again, but I don't think I can."

Amy smiled, resting her head on my hand. "I am tired today, but you aren't doing anything. I want to be here as much as you want me here."

"Good. But we'll go to bed early tonight, and I want you to nap on the weekend. I have nothing major planned except time alone with you."

Her lips quirked. "Nothing major? No sex marathons? How disappointing."

I leaned close and kissed her. "*That* isn't major for us. It's normal. I am going to keep you naked and in bed as much as I can."

"Good to know."

Amy gazed out of the window, enraptured. I stood behind her, looping my arms around her waist and pulling her close.

"It's breathtaking," she observed.

The view was spectacular. Vast and wild. Nothing but ocean for miles, the movement of the water constant. The waves crashed against the bluff, the sound hypnotic and soothing.

"I only stayed in the hotel the time I came. I didn't expect this."

"This" was the honeymoon cottage, but I had booked it for us. Separate from the main hotel and other cottages on the property, it was totally private. Meals could be catered, brought directly to the cabin, or you could eat in the dining room. Champagne and a delicious-looking platter of snacks had been set out for us. Fresh flowers were in the rooms. A large fireplace, fluffy towels, and a big bed waited. An outdoor hot tub protected by a cedar gazebo sat outside the master bedroom. The view could be seen from all the windows, the place built to take full advantage of the offering.

We'd been greeted by the owners, Dylan and Alexis Maxwell. They were welcoming and courteous and had driven us over to the cottage in the golf cart, her chatting and friendly. She told us the story of the bluff and the cabin and how they met, Dylan adding a comment or two. He was from Toronto and had moved here the same as I did, although their meeting was far more interesting than Amy's and mine, even though I was certain we were hearing the PG version. Dylan was quieter but still pleasant. It was obvious he adored his wife, by the way he looked at her, his stern countenance softening every time he did. It was much the same as the way Evan looked at Holly or I looked at Amy. I recognized the infatuated expression.

They made sure we were happy, then departed, telling us there was a cocktail hour at the main hotel every evening from four to six if we wanted to join them. From the way Amy and Alex, as she insisted we call her, chatted, I had a feeling we would end up there tomorrow, as long as Mia was still okay. She, Holly, and Angela would be heading to the party soon, and Holly promised to watch out for her, although I wasn't overly worried. Mia liked her friends, was excited about the thought of a sleepover with them and, with Holly and Angela there, wouldn't feel strange.

"What do you want to do first, Chippy? Explore? Have a snack? Get naked in the hot tub?" I asked, hoping for the latter.

She laughed. "How about a quick walk, then the hot tub?"

"Perfect." I wrapped my hand around hers. "Let's go."

It was a short walk to the main building, and we explored the many different aspects they had to offer. The resort had both an indoor and outdoor pool. Several hot tubs. I picked up a brochure, describing all the activities in the different seasons.

"We should bring Mia here in the winter. She loves to cross-country ski. I taught her last year."

Amy peered over my shoulder. "Oh, they have nightly bonfires. Even in the winter. That would be fun."

"And family cabins," I mused. "We should definitely plan it."

"I'll ask Alex about it later."

We walked back to the cabin as the sun began to sink. Amy shivered, and I grinned down at her.

"Ready for the hot tub, Chippy?"

"Yes."

"Awesome."

Ten minutes later, we sat in the swirling water, the steam vapors in the air around us. The view was equally beautiful from this spot, but even more so because of the woman beside me. Amy sat facing the edge of the hot tub, her arms draped over the side. Her skin glistened in the fading light, the solar lights dotting the landscape casting shadows around the tub. I handed her a glass of champagne and kissed her bare shoulder.

"It's so beautiful here," she whispered. "Thank you for bringing me."

"My pleasure."

She peeked over her shoulder at me. I was relaxed in the corner, enjoying the heat and bubbles. The view. The spectacle of her. She was far lovelier than the vista. Far lovelier than anything else I could think of. Her hair was up, exposing her neck. Her tattoo was bright against her creamy skin. She was sensuous in her simple beauty, making my body ache with desire. I smiled at her, taking a sip of champagne. She pushed off the edge, drifting closer. I tugged her to my lap, and she straddled me, our bodies aligning, slick and warm. I kissed her, our tongues stroking together in a slow dance of desire. Her nipples hardened against my chest, rubbing on my skin.

"Your pleasure," she whispered, ghosting her lips along my jaw to my ear. "I want to feel your pleasure, Simon. I want to feel all of it."

"I want to give it to you."

She met my eyes as I tipped up my glass and gave her a sip of champagne. She gasped as I poured the last mouthful down her neck and followed it with my tongue. I set my glass on the edge of the tub and grasped her hips, pulling her down and letting her feel me.

"Hold tight, Chippy. This is gonna be a wild ride."

"Perfect."

I covered her mouth with mine, kissing her passionately. The cold air touched my shoulders and neck as I angled my head to go as deeply as I could into her sweet mouth. She tasted like champagne and Amy—a heady combination. She wrapped her arms around my neck, the heat of the water dissipating quickly in the night air. She moaned as I shifted, lifting her, then sliding inside her. The heat between us was intense. The steam from the water, the breeze that came off the ocean, the feel of her skin, some hot, some cold, all were distinct yet intertwined.

And the feeling of her. Of us. There was nothing like it. I would never tire of it. Never get enough.

Amy grasped the edge of the hot tub and began moving herself up and down. I gripped her hips, guiding her, making sure to hit her clit as we came together. I sucked at her cold nipples, listening to her gasps and moans, groaning her name. She began to go faster, her cries louder. I pulled her flush to me, cold and hot once again meeting and merging. I thrust hard and fast, feeling her tighten around me. She buried her face in my neck, muffling the low scream that burst from her lips. I slid my hand into her hair, holding her close as I bucked wildly, my orgasm cresting high and hot, and I succumbed to the mind-numbing intensity of it.

We stilled, and I slid from the seat to the bottom of the tub, submerging us both. Amy sputtered a little, coughing and laughing.

"Don't drown me, Simon."

"Better a little unwanted water down your throat than frostbite, Chippy."

"Play your cards right, I'll have something else down my throat later," she mumbled.

I began to laugh, and I kissed her. "I'll hold you to that."

She grinned up at me. "You will, will you?"

I traced her lips with my finger. "I do love how this mouth of yours feels on my cock."

She bit my finger, and her eyes widened at the sensation of my cock beginning to lengthen again.

"Seriously, Simon, you need to have a talk with him. How can you possibly be ready to go again?"

"The promise of your mouth did it. Me talking to him will do nothing. But an in-depth conversation with you might do the trick."

She wrapped her hand around me. "Or make it worse," she said with a grin.

"We'll never know until we try."

She eyed the cedar deck on the hot tub. "Outside or in, Simon?"

The thought of her hot mouth around my cock while the rest of my body was cold somehow turned me on. I looked at her with a grin. "Can you make it fast?"

"Baby, you know I can."

"Frostbite, here I come."

Saturday was spent exploring the town. Doing some shopping. Amy amazed me. She looked at local crafts, helped me pick a stunning black-and-white photo for my bedroom. The dark clouds and shadows on the water were highlighted by the whitecaps between them. It was a large, striking piece.

"That would look perfect on the wall across from your bed," Amy mused.

I bent low and kissed her ear. "Our bed."

She shivered.

I bought it.

Not once did she ask me to buy her something. There were no hints, no long looks or exaggerated sighs. Her only demand was a cup of coffee and a shared piece of cake at a small bakery. I told her how refreshing it was to be with her. She tilted her head, studying me.

"Kelsey did a number on you, didn't she?"

"Yeah. And I'm sorry. I shouldn't compare you. It's night and day. And in case you don't realize it, Chippy—you're the light, not the darkness."

Still, I snuck a couple of purchases I planned to give her later. We bought Mia a pair of fuzzy slippers that looked like boots and a pretty new coat for the winter. It was floral with a big hood and an extra lining that could be taken out, although Amy assured me she would need it for the upcoming weather.

We went to the happy hour, visiting with some other couples staying at the resort and Alex and Dylan. Their children were there, their daughter reminding me of Mia. She adored Dylan, and the feeling was mutual. It was nice to see another father and daughter as close as Mia and I were. I was surprised when Alex told me Dylan was the girl's stepdad.

"But that doesn't matter to either of them," she said, her love-filled gaze on them. "They belong to each other."

"It's that way for Amy with my daughter," I agreed.

"Then she's a keeper."

I met Amy's eyes across the room with a smile.

"Yeah, she is."

We ate dinner in the cabin, the meal set up by the staff at the table overlooking the water. The food was incredible, and we were relaxed and content. Mia had loved her sleepover and was having a great time with Evan and Holly, so our worries were groundless. When I called earlier, she talked fast and hung up, anxious to get back to her day. I was thrilled to know how well she was doing. After dinner, we sat in the hot tub again, the temperature far too cold to be adventuresome, but we made up for it in front of the fireplace later.

On Sunday morning, it was hard to leave the resort, but we had to return to reality. I had accomplished exactly what I wanted. Time alone with Amy. We talked, laughed, made love over and over again, and enjoyed the beauty of the cottage and the peace of being just us. I somehow fell even deeper in love than I had been when we arrived. We were closer than ever. Set in our relationship and going forward. It made leaving easier. I made a silent promise to myself to bring Mia and Amy here in the winter. It would be a nice break, and they would enjoy themselves.

Our trip to Ontario was only two weeks away, and we chatted about it on the drive back home. Everyone was excited, and all of us were looking forward to the family adventure.

I smiled as I pulled into the driveway and Mia ran from the house, waving excitedly.

"Welcome home, Amy," I murmured. "Someone is excited to see us."

She sighed. "Now the weekend is perfect."

I fell a little more.

CHAPTER FIFTEEN

SIMON

T he time flew by, and before I knew it, we were on an airplane, headed to Ontario.

I leaned over the armrest, looking across the aisle. "How you doing, girls?"

Angela and Mia turned their heads with big grins. "Good." Then promptly went back to the movie they were watching. In front of us, Holly was sipping a ginger ale, Brandon asleep in his seat, and across the aisle, Evan was watching the same movie as the girls with Hannah.

I relaxed back, smiling at Amy. "You okay, Chippy?"

"I've never traveled business class before," she said, sipping the mimosa the flight attendant had given her.

I chuckled. "Compared to most planes, this is tiny. Usually, it's bigger with more services, but it's a short flight and a smaller plane." I stretched out my legs. "But still more comfortable."

I had booked us business class, rented a large SUV, and reserved the two big suites for the weekend. The rooms adjoined, and we had four bedrooms, two living spaces, plus kitchenettes. The resort had a huge indoor splash pool, hot tubs, tons of activities for the kids, and some adult ones as well. Everyone had been excited about the trip, and no one complained when we had to be at the airport at five a.m. I hoped that meant the kids would be in bed early tonight. I'd booked dinner for eight o'clock and arranged the in-room childcare, but given the earliness of the hour we'd left, plus how Mia had barely slept, I had a feeling they'd all be asleep by seven.

"The girls are so excited," Amy murmured.

"I'm looking forward to the weekend. I'll spend the day in meetings, then I'm yours the rest of the time. You ladies have spa treatments booked this afternoon, and Evan and Brandon are going to hang by the pool. We'll do the family dinner tonight. Saturday morning is Niagara Falls, and the afternoon and evening are filled with activities at the lodge. The kids will have a blast. I arranged late checkout on Sunday."

Amy leaned over, kissing my cheek. "This is the best gift ever."

I smiled and stroked her cheek. She'd been worried about getting the day off, but it had been arranged and I'd made the plans around her time frame. I would get them settled at the hotel, then head off for my meetings. I wanted the trip to be longer, but I knew it was hard for her to take time off as a teacher. Luckily, we were able to arrange the one day ahead of time.

I laced our fingers together, leaning over the seat and whispering in her ear. "Lots of couples get married in the Falls, Chippy. You want to join them?"

She laughed, rolling her eyes and ignoring me.

"Leave as Amy McNeil, come back as Amy Fletcher."

"We don't have a license, Simon," she pointed out sensibly.

"Damn."

She turned, meeting my eyes. "One day," she whispered. "One day, I would love to be Mrs. Simon Fletcher."

My breath caught. "Yeah?"

She nodded. "But not today."

I kissed her again. "I can live with that."

The flight was uneventful, the drive to the lodge smooth, although the kids were fascinated by the number of cars on the road with us. Angela and Hannah had never seen so many vehicles at once, and they had a lot of fun with Evan and his I Spy game that kept them entertained. Even Brandon got in on the action, pointing his chubby finger in all directions and imitating the girls.

I hated leaving them, even for a short while. But the car I'd hired was waiting, and I went back into Toronto, using the time to work while the chauffeur dealt with the traffic. Looking around, I recalled when this was normal. Thousands of cars, endless people, smog, bumper-to-bumper traffic—and the noise. I had been used to it when I lived here, but being away and in a small town brought the reality of the chaos I had left behind into focus. It swept away any lingering doubts I'd had about moving to Nova Scotia.

My meetings were back-to-back, but successful. I soothed some worried minds, met with some new clients, and touched base with some other businesspeople I had dealings with. I had arranged the meetings in a room close to the highway and instructed the driver to use the 407 on the way back. The large toll added to the bill was worth the time it saved being stuck in traffic. By the end of the day, I was anxious to get back to my family and start enjoying myself with them.

Over dinner, Holly and Amy made plans for the next day. They had both wanted to see Niagara Falls and knew the kids would love it.

"Okay, so we'll go in the morning before they get really busy. We can see the Falls, do the boat ride, the Ferris wheel, then lunch and back to the lodge," Amy said. "The kids can do the pool and the play stuff, and there is the scavenger hunt at three. We can sit and relax since it is supervised. Then it's dinner and movie night for them."

"And we get to go out on the town," I interjected. "We have reservations at nine at the Skylon. You can see the view of the Falls at night. The food is spectacular, I've been told."

"That sounds amazing."

I glanced over at Mia, trying not to laugh. She was nodding off, the hamburger she'd ordered still clutched in her hand. Beside her, Angela wasn't faring much better, and Hannah and Brandon were both passed out.

"I think the kids are down."

Holly chuckled. "They've been going like crazy all day. The pool, the maze, the games, back in the pool. Nonstop. I'm not surprised."

Evan groaned. "They'll be up at the crack of dawn tomorrow if we let them sleep." But he leaned over, taking the burger from Mia's hand and settling her against the back of the leather bench so her neck didn't get stiff. "Let them sleep."

I smiled indulgently and picked up my scotch. "Yeah. They've had a busy day."

Amy slipped her hand into mine, squeezing it. "A great day."

"Good."

The kids were enraptured by Niagara Falls. Mesmerized by the rush of the water. The mist that swirled around us. They had been up early, and Evan and I had taken them downstairs for breakfast, letting Holly and Amy sleep in. Once that was done, we bundled them into the car and headed for the Falls. It was early so not as busy as usual, which was nice. We did all the touristy things, but the kids liked the Ferris wheel the best, exclaiming in delight over the views and wanting to go back to the Falls again. We stopped for coffee, sitting by the window so they could watch the water, then took them on the boat ride that went close to the Falls. They squealed as the wind swirled the water at the boat and we all got drenched. Brandon crowed in delight, held safe in Evan's arms. Amy and I held Mia and Angela tight, and Holly kept Hannah close, all of us enjoying the thrill of the ride.

We were laughing and shaking our damp hair as we headed back to the van, ready to return to the lodge. I carried a bag of souvenirs we'd paid far too much money for, but the kids loved. The girls each had a stuffed bear, and Brandon had chosen a dinosaur as his new toy. All were emblazoned with the Niagara Falls logo, and they were excited about them. I was relaxed, happy, and thrilled at how the weekend was going.

Until my name was spoken. Loudly. "Simon?"

I stopped walking, instantly recognizing that annoyed, haughty voice.

I turned and met the frosty gaze of my ex-wife.

"Simon?" she repeated, then she frowned as she took in our group. "*Evan*? Is that you? What are you doing here together?"

"Amy," I murmured, tightening my grip on her hand in warning. "You and Holly take the kids to the van. We'll be right there."

Amy squeezed my hand in understanding. Holly turned to Evan, who looked down at her, pressing a kiss to her forehead. "Go," he murmured.

"Who is that lady?" I heard Mia ask as they hurried away.

"I don't know," Amy lied, knowing full well who was in front of me but wanting to protect Mia. "Let's have a race to the van! Winner gets another piece of fudge!"

I waited until I heard their footsteps fade then drew in a deep breath. "Kelsey."

Evan said nothing.

She looked between us. "Why are you here together?"

"That's none of your business."

She looked over my shoulder, an amused smirk on her face. "Isn't that sweet," she said, the sarcasm evident. "My ex and my brother. What are you— besties now? Did you bond over your shared dislike of me? Here with your families, having a little vacation? How wonderful." She clapped her hands, the saccharine sound of her fake delight grating on my nerves. "Was Mia one of them?" she asked. "I should go say hello to my daughter. How rude of you not to introduce us, Simon."

I studied the woman I had married, wondering how I had been fooled by her. She was beautiful— there was no doubt of that—but her beauty was only skin-deep. Underneath, she was bitter, angry. Filled with disdain for those around her. As I'd discovered, she was selfish and cared only for herself.

"If you need an introduction to your own child, then it's best left alone," Evan said.

"Stay out of this," Kelsey snapped.

Evan crossed his arms. "No, I don't think so. I'm too fond of my niece to let you even get close to her."

"You can't stop me. I want to see her."

"You've never had any interest in her, so why would I bother introducing you?" I narrowed my eyes. "And why are *you* here?" Kelsey wasn't one for a weekend in Niagara Falls. She would rather fly to Barbados or somewhere far more exotic.

"A wedding. Clichéd but I had to come. An investor for my business."

"So, you're marrying them or just fleecing them?" I asked, unable to contain my snark. "Did you find yet another man to sink your claws into for his money?"

She smiled—a cold, calculated smile. "Well, since your last missive from your lawyer refused me any money, I had to look elsewhere."

"And you will have to continue. You're not getting another penny from me. I'm done with you, Kelsey."

She glanced over my shoulder. "I think I'll go see Mia."

I couldn't bear to hear that name come from her mouth. I grabbed her arm as she tried to go past me. "No, you will not."

"I'm her mother. I have rights."

"You gave birth to her, then abandoned her. You are *not* her mother. You gave up those rights years ago. She doesn't want to know you. She has zero interest in you."

She tilted her head, shaking off my grip. "I watched you for a few moments," she hissed. "Playing the happy family with your little girlfriend and our daughter. Hanging out with my loser brother." She shook her head. "I had such hopes for you, Simon. Such a disappointment."

I laughed. "Do you really think your opinion means anything to me, Kelsey? Or to Evan? Neither of us cares. Go back to your empty life. Leave us alone. Leave Mia alone. You are not welcome in her life."

"Maybe I've changed my mind. Maybe I'll ask for some visitation."

I refused to let her see the fear her words caused me. I didn't want her anywhere close to my daughter. "You signed away your parental rights. I'll refuse."

She batted her eyelashes. "I was confused. Lost and hurt over my broken marriage. I fought so hard to keep her, and I've been missing her for five years. I'll plead my case to a judge."

Evan began to laugh. "Nice try, you coldhearted witch. Your daughter is eight, not five. I bet you don't even remember her birthday."

Anger showed her true nature. She wasn't so beautiful when she was glaring, the frown lines evident under the skillful makeup. "Some money would keep me quiet and away. I'd stay busy with my business."

I was disgusted by her statement. "Stay busy with whatever you want. But not in my life and certainly not in Mia's. Go away, Kelsey. I have nothing to say to you, and I'm not interested in whatever you have to say. Let's go, Evan."

We began to walk away, and she called out, "We'll talk soon, Simon. You know I won't let this go."

I refused to turn. To let her get to me.

I kept walking.

CHAPTER SIXTEEN

SIMON

We were quiet in the van, Amy holding my hand all the way back to the lodge. It wasn't until the kids were busy with the scavenger hunt and we were sitting around a table by the pool watching them that Evan spoke.

"I'm sorry, Simon."

"You have nothing to be sorry for."

"My sister is an awful person."

"Again, not your fault." I shook my head. "I can't believe of all the places to run into her, it would be in Niagara Falls. She always hated this place. But then again, she hated everything, so I guess she ran out of places to go."

Amy met my eyes. "Do you think she meant what she said? About Mia?"

I had told her what Kelsey said as the kids got ready to go for a swim. Amy assured me Mia didn't get a good look at Kelsey and hadn't recognized her. Nor had she heard anything that upset her.

"No. They were empty threats. She has zero interest in my daughter. She never has. She resented being pregnant. She didn't want to be a real mother—she liked to say she had a child, but she wanted none of the responsibilities." I sipped my coffee. "She got pregnant to keep me, and after she had me where she wanted me, I saw her true colors. I was horrified at what I had trapped myself into, but I wanted to be there for Mia. Kelsey fought me for custody to punish me. Her lawyer was sleazy and seemed to enjoy making me suffer as much as Kelsey did. She didn't want Mia. When she finally got tired of it all, she offered me a divorce with full parental rights for a big cash payout. I was relieved, and I jumped at the chance. She doesn't want to be a part of Mia's life. She wants more money."

Evan leaned forward with a frown. "Will you give it to her?"

"No. I already contacted my lawyer and told him what was going on. Halton is on it. He'll get in touch with her lawyer and make my position clear. He'll keep her away." I huffed an annoyed sound. "I guess she's bled the other husbands dry too."

Evan shook his head. "I was cut out of the will, my brother drank himself to an early death in a DUI, and she's the only beneficiary now. I heard my father died and my mother isn't well. I'm sure Kelsey is waiting for that payout."

"How sad to live that way," Amy murmured.

I picked up her hand and kissed it. "Something you'd know nothing about, Chippy. That's why I love you so much."

She smiled and cupped my cheek. "Has this ruined the day?"

"No, I refuse to let it. Mia isn't affected, and I will not let that woman ruin this weekend. I'm going to put it out of my mind and enjoy the rest of the day with my family."

Evan nodded. "Good plan."

Angela came over, holding Brandon's hand. "Mommy, Brandon fell."

Holly bent, scooping him up. He showed her his scraped knee and she kissed it, fussing over him. He snuggled into her arms, content to stay while Angela ran back and joined Mia and Hannah. Evan leaned close, running his hand over Brandon's head, chuckling as his son began to nod off.

"He always wants to do whatever the girls are doing. Another year and he can keep up, but he's still a baby."

"Big boy, Daddy," Brandon protested sleepily.

"Not too big yet," Evan responded. "Not yet."

Holly shifted, and Evan held out his arms. "I'll take him. I know your back is a little sore today."

"You okay?" I asked her.

Holly smiled. "Yeah, I'm fine. Just getting to the point where my regular clothes don't fit, my shape is changing, and my back aches a bit. Holding him isn't as easy as it was with the way he grows."

She stood. "I think I'll go have a nap before dinner."

Evan glanced my way, and I grinned. "Go with your wife. We'll watch the kids."

He grinned back. "Thanks. I'll put my boy down and tuck my wife in. Maybe grab a little nap myself."

I chuckled as I watched them walk away. "No nap is happening right away," I murmured, meeting Amy's gaze and winking.

She grinned. "Well, they watched the kids while we 'grabbed a shower' this morning. Only fair."

I laughed and stood. "Let's go play in the pool with the girls."

She sprang to her feet. "Race you!"

I chased after her, hoping for a reward if I caught her.

Another game I liked.

"Oh my God, the view is spectacular," Amy breathed out, her gaze filled with wonder. "Look at all the lights. So…magical."

"I know," Holly agreed. "It is."

I loved seeing the wonder on their faces. Especially Amy's. She loved new things and adventures. I enjoyed watching her reactions.

She was beautiful tonight. Her hair was caught up

in a cascade of curls over one shoulder. Her lacy blouse was a pale green, and the skirt she wore had a jagged hem and swirled around her knees. She wore leather ankle boots and had laughed when I'd kissed her in the elevator, telling her she looked like a pirate wench and I planned on ravishing her later with the sexy boots on. Her eyes lit up at my suggestion, and it thrilled me to know she was as crazy about me as I was about her. And we synched physically as well. She was sexy and unique, and I loved that about her.

I caught her eye and leaned close, brushing a kiss to her cheek. "You're the magical one, Chippy. In case I forgot to tell you, you're stunning tonight."

She blushed softly, the pink highlighting her cheeks.

"You look pretty damn stunning yourself."

I picked up my scotch with a wry smirk. "I feel pretty waterlogged, to be honest."

Everyone laughed. I had spent over two hours with the girls in the pool. Amy played for a while, sat in the hot tub, relaxed on the edge of the water, acting as judge for the races the girls kept having. I was the referee, the one to be dunked, the shoulders they wanted to ride on. It was fun but exhausting, and I swore I had swallowed half the water in the pool between the splashes and the dunking. I deserved the expensive scotch I had ordered.

But it had been a good time and took my mind off Kelsey. I refused to allow her appearance to ruin this weekend, and I purposefully pushed her out of my mind. She didn't deserve to be part of this family time.

I perused the menu. "What looks good?"

"Everything," Holly replied. "I'm starving. The appetizers sound so delicious, I don't know which one to pick."

"Then let's order a bunch and share."

She grinned widely. "Perfect."

We strolled along the sidewalk, the streets still busy with the crisp late fall air around us. I tucked Amy into my side as we stood, looking over the Falls. They were lit up, the colors changing constantly. The roar of the water and the power of the movement was mesmerizing.

"Thank you for this weekend," she murmured, tightening her arm around my waist.

I bent and pressed a kiss to her head. Beside us, Evan and Holly were wrapped around each other, admiring the view.

Dinner had been delicious, and we'd all eaten far too much. I'd had two large scotches, and Evan and Amy shared a bottle of red. Holly had a couple of sips, but otherwise stuck to tonic water and lime. We'd finished off the dinner with a decadent array of desserts and decided we needed the exercise so chose to walk for a while before getting a cab to the lodge.

Knowing I was going to drink, we'd chosen to leave the van there to be safe.

"I came here once at Christmas. The light displays were incredible. Maybe we can do that one year," I said. I had a feeling a lot of family trips were in the future for us. We got along well and enjoyed one another's company. Plus, the kids were such good friends, I could see this happening a lot. The thought pleased me.

Holly nodded. "I used to take the bus out and walk around close to Christmas with a couple of friends. It was amazing."

"We'll plan it when your current bun is done and walking." I winked at her.

She grinned. "Your own might be cooking by then."

I met Amy's eyes, and a silent conversation flowed. We both liked that idea—very much.

Holly's grin got wider as she looked between us. "Or sooner."

I tucked Amy close. "Or sooner," I agreed.

We all looked back at the lights.

Smiling.

The next morning, Amy closed her bag. "Ready."

Mia grimaced. "I can't get my zipper to work."

Laughing, Amy leaned over and helped her.

"That's because you bought so many things yesterday," she teased. "Your suitcase is bursting!"

Mia giggled.

"I think the rainbow unicorn is the cause," I added. She had seen the overly large "stuffie," as she called him, in the gift shop, and I couldn't resist buying him for her. She rarely asked for things, and I enjoyed spoiling her on occasion.

"But Daddy, he was so cute!"

I ruffled her hair. "I know, Sweet Pea."

She flung her arms around my legs, hugging me. "I had the best time, Daddy! It was so much fun."

I bent and lifted her into my arms, hugging her close. I was grateful Kelsey hadn't even registered with Mia or confused her. "I'm glad. You ready to go home?"

"Yep!"

I set her on her feet, and she ran to see the girls. I turned to Amy. "You ready, Chippy?"

"Yes."

I stepped closer. "Are you coming with us or going to your place?"

"To yours."

I kissed her. "Good answer."

The flight was uneventful. As we waited for our luggage, I sighed in relief as I looked around the small airport.

"I always thought I would live in Toronto," I mused. "But after being gone for a while, I am so glad

I don't. The people, the smog, the traffic…" I chuckled. "I had forgotten."

"I know what you mean," Evan agreed. "Once I lived here for a while, I never wanted to go back." He linked hands with Holly. "Although my one visit was certainly worth it."

"Think how many people's lives you changed because of that drive, Evan."

He nodded. "All because of a broken part and the sweetest angel helping me warm up." His gaze was soft as he looked at Holly. "I found my place because of her."

She smiled and leaned up on her toes to kiss him, then winked. "We both did."

He shook his head, clearing the memories, no doubt. "Anyway, it's a fun place to visit, but this is home."

I laced my fingers with Amy's and met her soft glance. "Yeah," I said. "It is."

We separated at our cars that we had left at the airport and headed to our respective homes.

"You need anything from your place?" I asked Amy.

"No. I packed an extra outfit for tomorrow. I'll pick up some more things after school."

I loved it every time I opened the closet and saw something else of hers hanging beside my clothes. Or cleared out more drawer space. The more things she left, the more we got to have her with us. Mia and I liked that a lot.

We got back into our routine quickly, except for one change. Amy stayed over more often. I missed her on the Thursday night while she had dinner with some friends and went back to her apartment. She called to say good night and see how we were. I smiled into the phone.

"I'm in bed, reading. Naked. You could come over and help me turn the pages, Chippy."

"Stop it. I've had wine, so I can't drive."

"Take a cab."

She laughed. "It's ten o'clock, Simon. Tell your dick to stand down and I'll take care of him tomorrow."

It was my turn to laugh. "He never stands down long around you. But my bed feels empty. And there isn't anyone running their cold feet on my legs to warm up."

"I'll make up for that. There's a cold front heading our way. I'll need lots of places warmed up."

"I'm your man."

"Yes, you are." She paused, and I knew she was getting ready to hang up. "I'll see you in the morning."

"Evan and Holly are taking Mia to school. I have a Zoom meeting first thing." I reminded her. "I'll see you after school."

"Okay. Good night, Simon. I love you."

Her words filled my heart.

"I love you."

CHAPTER SEVENTEEN

SIMON

My phone buzzed. Once. Again. Then again. I frowned, directing my gaze to the device sitting on the desk beside me. Seeing Evan's name, I held up my finger, interrupting my client.

"Sorry. Hold one moment, Larry. I think I have an urgent call here."

I muted him and answered the phone. "Evan?"

"Get to the school," Evan hissed. "Kelsey is here, and she is causing trouble."

I was on my feet in a second. "Larry, I have to get back to you. It's my daughter."

"Go," he said.

The six-minute drive seemed to take forever. I pulled up to the school, seeing a small group gathered at the front of the building, arguing. The entire school appeared to be on the one side, slowly making their way back into the building, and a fire truck was just leaving.

I raced over to the group at the front of the building, shocked at the sight before me.

Evan and Holly were with Amy, who was holding Mia, refusing to let her go. Two things hit me at once. The bright red handprint on Amy's face and the furious expression she wore. I had seen her annoyed. Upset. Disappointed. But never this angry.

The principal, Mrs. Bremmer, was there, with the small group of people around Mia. Kelsey stood, dressed as if she were attending a business meeting for socialites, her suit and heels out of place in this simple setting. Her hands were on her hips, and she was yelling. Off to the side stood another man, looking uncomfortable and confused.

"Give me my daughter."

"She is not your daughter," Amy snapped. "You have no place in her life."

I strode forward, pushing myself beside Mia and Amy. "What the hell is going on here?"

Mia lifted her face, her tearstained cheeks and red eyes hitting me in the gut. "Daddy, this lady keeps yelling. She tried to take me out of school. I don't like her!"

I took her from Amy, holding her close. "It's okay, Sweet Pea. Daddy's here." I focused on Kelsey. "What the hell game are you playing at?"

She tossed her hair, meeting my furious gaze. Her

eyes were red, the pupils dilated. "I just came to see my daughter. I was taking her out for breakfast."

"You have no right to take her anywhere."

"I'm her mother."

"You're nobody." I looked at the principal. "Has anyone called the police? I want her charged with attempted kidnapping."

Evan slid his phone from his pocket. "I'll call."

Kelsey paled. "You wouldn't."

Evan shook his head. "Watch me."

I leaned down, kissing Mia's head. "Baby, are you okay to go with Evan and Holly? They'll take you to their place, and I'll come soon, okay? We'll go home after."

"I don't have to go with her?" she whispered.

"No. Never."

"Okay."

I transferred her to Evan's embrace and waited as he and Holly took her to the car and left. I slid my arm around Amy's waist, tugging her close. "Are you all right?"

"I'm fine," she said through clenched teeth.

I touched her cheek. "She did this?"

"Yes."

I looked up, meeting Kelsey's angry gaze. "I'll add assault to the charges as well."

"I'm leaving," she informed me. "Come on, Robert."

I grabbed her arm. "You are going nowhere." I

looked at Mrs. Bremmer. "Is there a place we can go for some privacy?"

"Yes," she replied. "This way."

I heard Kelsey's voice through the door, the words unclear, but her tone annoyed. The police were questioning her. I ran a hand over my face as I told Halton, my lawyer, what had occurred.

"Fuck," he replied. "What an idiot. I'll crucify her for this, Simon."

"I want a court order that she never comes near Mia or me again. Get that done. I have no idea what harm she has caused to Mia. I know she hit Amy."

"Holy shit." He whistled lowly. "She's even crazier than she used to be. She's desperate. I ran a quick check. She is broke. Owes money left, right, and center. Her last husband went bankrupt, so she got nothing."

"I don't give a shit. She crossed the line today. Hit her with everything you've got, Halton."

He chuckled. "My pleasure."

I hung up and scrubbed my face.

What a mess. Mia's teacher, Mrs. Reynolds, had fallen and broken her leg this morning. With no substitute available, they had put the two classes together. A fire alarm went off, and while trying to get double the number of kids outside, Ms. Aldridge lost track of Mia. Kelsey was waiting and was trying to walk away with Mia when Amy spotted her. She ran after her, snatching Mia, who was struggling to get free. Kelsey had fought, slapping Amy, who refused to let Mia go. Evan and Holly had still been there and saw what was happening. They stepped in and Evan called me. The principal stood with them, and I showed up. The man with Kelsey was her latest sugar daddy, although I had a feeling after today, that relationship was toast.

I was furious at Kelsey, incensed that she had struck Amy, frightened Mia, and caused such a scene. She had somehow tagged along with someone else coming into the school, and she had been the one to pull the fire alarm as a distraction. I was horrified thinking of what would have happened if Kelsey had gotten away with it. If Amy hadn't seen her.

Amy appeared beside me, her cheek still red. She slipped her arm around me. "Simon, are you okay?"

"Am I okay?" I replied. "Baby, you're the one who confronted her. Saved Mia." I touched her bruising cheek. "Are you okay?"

"I will be. I want to go in there and give her a piece of my mind."

"I want to throw her ass in jail and let her rot. Halton is working it from his angle."

A police officer stepped out. I knew him and shook his hand. "Fred. I mean, Officer Baxter."

"Simon." He indicated the room with a jerk of his head. "What do you want done?"

"I want her in jail. My lawyer is going to have her charged."

"She's, ah…" He paused. "She's in bad shape."

"I don't care."

"She's high."

"What?"

"On what, I don't know. But she's on something."

I thought of her eyes. I felt sick to my stomach, knowing how close she'd come to getting her hands on Mia. To putting her in a car and driving away with her. I must have made a noise because Amy gripped my hand. "Calm, Simon."

"She is going to be charged with public mischief, endangering a child, assault, trespassing, plus whatever else your lawyer comes up with."

"I want to throw the book at her."

"I understand. I need you to come down to the station and file charges."

"Okay. I'll follow you in a few moments."

They led Kelsey out the back door, her boyfriend —or whatever he was—with them. I had no idea where he fit into all this, but I was going to find out. I spoke briefly with Mrs. Bremmer and Ms. Aldridge, who was upset and horrified that someone had almost taken a child away who was under her care. Her frosty, cold nature was replaced by one of genuine distress as she praised Amy and her quick response.

"All children should have someone who loves them so much," she said. "I apologize for my part in this."

I shook my head and extended my hand. "I don't

blame you, Ms. Aldridge. None of you. Kelsey is the one responsible. She caused all this uproar, and I am deeply sorry."

Both women assured me the children would be looked after, comforted, and spoken to. Luckily, with the way it happened and the people around them, most of the children saw nothing since the teachers kept them separate, and the firefighters and trucks distracted them from paying too much attention to what was happening around the corner. The women left, and I turned to Amy, pulling her into my arms.

"Thank God for you."

"Simon, she frightened me. The look in her eyes." She shivered. "I hate her for upsetting Mia."

"I hate that she touched you. I'm so angry I don't know how to handle it."

"I'm fine," she assured me.

"Can you leave?"

"Yes. I have an aide and a parent in today, and they can see to the kids. They can color and have a snack." She covered her cheek. "I don't want them to see me like this." She lifted her eyes to mine. "I'm going to cover it up at my place, then go to Holly's. I need to see Mia."

"Take her home, please. Wait for me. I'll be there as soon as possible." I bent and kissed her. "Thank you. You saved our girl."

"She is ours," she whispered, tears filling her eyes. "I love her like my own."

I kissed her again. "I know."

"This is the best thing," Halton assured me over the phone. "She'll be escorted to the plane, and I'll meet it here with her lawyer, and then she'll be taken right to the facility. That way, she is out of the province and away from Mia and you. She has agreed to plead guilty to avoid a trial. She'll sign the restraining order and go to rehab. She's also agreed to sign a document that she will never contact you again."

"Evan and his family either," I added with a sigh. "I really want her in jail."

"I know. But her freedom is being taken away, you get the court orders, and she now has a record, which limits her travel. When she gets out of rehab, she'll be under house arrest for a while and wear a tracking device on her ankle. Once all that is over, if she so much as appears across the road from you, all bets are off."

"Who is the guy with her?"

"An idiot in lust or love. But be grateful for him. He talked some sense into her. She told him a different story to get him to bring her there."

"Of course she did."

"The addiction to painkillers started after a car accident last year. He had no idea how bad it was. But he is sticking with her. Who knows—maybe this will be the guy who sets her straight."

"I don't really care. I just want her gone permanently."

"As much as I'd like to take her down in court, this is the best way. Mia and Amy aren't involved. You get what you want, at least for the most part. And you can leave and go home to your girls. I know you're anxious to do so."

I rubbed the back of my head. Halton was right. "Fine," I conceded. "Make it happen. Get her out of here and do the deal."

"Consider it handled. Today is the last day you'll ever hear from Kelsey."

"Thanks, Halton."

"You got it." He hung up, and after speaking with the officer in charge, I signed some papers and headed home.

I wasn't sure what I would find when I got there, but Mia and Amy were curled up on the sofa, a bowl of popcorn between them and *Finding Nemo* playing. I watched them from the doorway for a moment. Mia was tucked into Amy's side, a grin on her face as she watched the movie. Amy was stroking Mia's head absently, her face pale but clear, the makeup she'd applied covering the mark Kelsey had left.

I strode forward. "There're my girls."

Mia looked up. "Daddy! We're watching Dory."

I bent and kissed her. "What a surprise."

She smiled, not looking upset or worried. I breathed a small sigh of relief. Amy looked calm, accepting my kiss to her uninjured cheek. Her eyes were worried, but she smiled. "All okay?"

"Yep. I'll tell you all about it later."

Mia turned her attention back to the screen, and I lifted my eyebrows in a silent question to Amy, who shrugged and nodded. I settled on Mia's other side, and she wiggled to get the perfect position between us, her focus on the movie. I looked over at Amy, seeing the edges of the mark under the makeup, and my anger built again. She slid her fingers between mine, squeezing my hand and shaking her head.

"Hungry?" she inquired. "I made you a sandwich. It's in the fridge."

"Yeah, I could eat."

"Daddy, can we have pizza tonight?" Mia asked.

"Sure, Sweet Pea. If that's what you want."

She nodded, still focused on the screen. "With extra cheese and pepperonis."

"Okay."

The movie finished as I ate the sandwich Amy made me and drank a cup of coffee. Amy stood, smoothing down her shirt. "I have a few things to do. I'll be in my office."

She left, and I noticed the way Mia's eyes followed her and the frown on her face. I turned to her on the sofa and tucked a long wave of hair behind her ear. "You wanna talk, Sweet Pea?"

"What about?"

"What happened today. I know you must have questions. I know it was scary, and I want to make sure you're okay," I said gently.

"I was scared. But I saw Amy, and I knew it would

be okay. Uncle E explained some stuff to me, so I get it, Daddy."

"What stuff?"

"He said that lady was my biologe mother."

"Biological," I corrected.

"Yeah. He said she was in a bad mood and wanted to cause trouble. He told me she just wanted to take me for breakfast. But if she hadn't been so rushed, I could have told her I'd *had* breakfast. She isn't good at listening." She shook her head. "It's not nice to grab people and try to take them for breakfast if they aren't hungry. It's just *rude*." She sounded indignant.

"No, it's not nice. Did she hurt you, Sweet Pea? Hold your arm too tight?"

She pulled up her sleeve. "No. Uncle E checked and kissed it better in case, but it's fine."

"Good thing for Uncle E."

"He told me he'd like to give her a taste of her own medicine, but she didn't have any medicine so I didn't know what he meant."

"Um, he was saying she wasn't nice."

"He said she was like that their whole life. That she didn't like him. How can you not like Uncle E?"

"I know."

Mia shook her head. "My sister won't be like that. She'll be like Amy, 'cause Amy'll be her biologe. And I'll look after her."

I didn't correct her this time—or comment on the sister part.

"Sometimes people aren't good like you are," I explained.

"That's what Uncle E said. He's nice, but his sister wasn't. He had a brother too who was mean. Isn't it great we got Uncle E and he is so awesome?"

"It is."

"I'm glad Amy was there. But it made me mad that the lady yelled and tried to hit Amy. Amy said she missed and hit her shoulder. That is very bad. You don't hit people."

I was grateful Mia hadn't seen the slap. That Evan had talked to her and made the whole thing seem like an encounter with a grumpy person. I hoped there would be no lasting effects on my daughter because of Kelsey.

"You're right. You never hit. I'm glad Amy was there too. And I promise that lady—"

She interrupted me. "Kelsey. Uncle E said her name was Kelsey."

"Yes, it is. I promise you Kelsey will never bother you again."

"Good. Can I go back to school on Monday?"

"Yes."

"I like it there. I like it here—especially if Kelsey isn't around."

"You'll never have to see her again."

"Okay." She shifted closer. "But Daddy, I wanna talk about Amy."

I pulled her onto my lap, holding her close. "What about her, Sweet Pea?"

"She was a real mom today. Like Holly. She protected me. Yelled at Kelsey. Held me really tight."

"I know."

"I want her to be my mom, and I asked Uncle E how to make it happen."

"I see. And what did Uncle E say?"

"He said you had to do three things. So you need to do them, okay?"

"What are the three things?"

She held up her fingers, counting down. "You have to ask her to marry you." Then she frowned. "Wait, first you have to buy a ring. That's the number one rule. Then you ask her. When she says yes, then you have to make it legal. And ask her to be my mom." She paused. "Or maybe you ask her to be my mom when you ask her to marry you."

"I think I can figure it out."

"He said something about you have to man up, but I don't know what that means. Maybe you need help to do all that?"

My lips quirked. "Ah, no. I got it."

"Good. I really want her to be my mom. And I want a sister. You can have a brother for me later, but I really want a sister first."

"How about we start with the ring and the question first?"

"Soon?"

"You'd like that, Mia?"

She nodded. "We need Amy, Daddy. I need a mommy, and you need a wife."

"Why do you think that, baby?" I asked, curious. "We were always okay when it was just us."

"Because she makes your heart show in your eyes, Daddy. I like it when I see your heart."

I blinked at her words.

"Then I better get busy."

She nodded. "Get a nice ring, Daddy."

I kissed the end of her nose. "I'll do that. Can you keep it a secret until I ask her?"

"Yes."

I tucked her tight to my chest. "I love you, Mia."

She flung her arms around my neck. "I love you, Daddy."

We had pizza and watched another movie. All of us wore pajamas and warm socks and snuggled under the blanket, Mia tucked between us. I saw Amy glance at her often. The glimmer of tears happened a few times, and I held her hand, squeezing her fingers. Mia was happy, sipping her juice, eating her pizza, stealing the pepperoni off mine as usual. She fell asleep between us, and neither Amy nor I moved to carry her upstairs, even after the movie ended.

"Are you all right, Amy?" I asked, seeing the way she looked at Mia.

She nodded, but once again, her eyes filled with tears.

"She's fine," I whispered. "Evan did a great job talking to her, and she is okay. I'll watch her."

"I don't know if I'm okay," she whispered back. "I knew I loved her. I knew she was so special to me, but when I saw Kelsey and the way she was dragging her away, something just snapped."

I caressed her cheek. "Your momma bear came out. Evan said you were ferocious. Standing your ground, telling Kelsey off. Refusing to release Mia. Protecting her."

"I couldn't bear to let her touch her. Just thinking of what might have happened if I had been two minutes longer coming outside…" She covered her face and began to weep silently. I stood, taking Mia with me and settling her into the corner of the sofa. I sat next to Amy and pulled her into my arms, letting her cry. I ran my hands up and down her back, making hushing noises the way I did when Mia was upset, but I didn't try to stop her tears. I let her cry it out, then pressed some tissues into her hand, and once she lifted her gaze to mine, I cupped her face. The tears had washed away some of the makeup, and I saw the faint outline of the bruise Kelsey had left behind. I kissed her skin gingerly, not wanting to hurt her at all.

"You *were* there," I murmured. "You stopped Kelsey. She will never come near Mia again. Or you. Any of us. Halton texted and said she's under watch in rehab. She's signed everything and will have a record now. She's out of our life for good."

She nodded, a silent shiver running through her.

"Thank you for protecting our girl today, Amy. I have the same images of Kelsey getting away with it, but it didn't happen. We can't think about the what-ifs but celebrate the reality we have. Mia is safe, slightly annoyed at the rudeness of a woman she has no desire to know, and she is with us. Where she is gonna stay. Okay?"

"Okay."

"How about we go to bed?"

"Can Mia sleep with us?"

I chuckled. "Yeah, she can. For tonight. I don't want her to think something is wrong, though. I want to carry on as if things are normal so she doesn't feed off our fears, okay?"

"I know."

I kissed her softly. "I'll bring her up. You go get ready."

She walked up the stairs, and I gazed after her in wonder. I had no idea how I'd gotten lucky enough to find her, but I wasn't letting her go.

Evan was right. Time to man up.

It was ring shopping time.

CHAPTER EIGHTEEN

SIMON

A few days later, I walked into the local coffee shop, smiling at the greeting of the owner.

"Simon Fletcher," Gladys called out. "Out and about today?"

"Errands," I replied.

"Not going so well from the look on your face. Need a coffee?"

"And a sandwich, please."

"The usual?"

I wondered if I would ever get used to that line. In Toronto, I was never asked if I wanted "the usual." Places were simply too busy to keep track of that sort of thing, and no matter how often I frequented my local coffee haunt, no one ever remembered me. Here, it was different. Everyone knew you. Remembered you. I loved it.

"Please. Extra pickles today. I need the treat."

Gladys laughed. "You got it. Sit. I'll bring you coffee."

I sat down heavily in the end booth, which was my favorite place to sit here. I could see the restaurant and watch the activity on the street out the window at the same time. It was a small town, but it was bustling. People coming and going, getting on with their daily tasks. Tourists wandering and discovering the many little shops. We had a nice pace here.

Gladys slid a steaming cup of coffee in front of me. A moment later, a corned beef on rye with hot mustard and a pile of her homemade garlic pickles on the side was placed on the table.

"That'll make your day better."

I winked at her. "You know it."

I relaxed back in the booth, eating my sandwich, sipping my coffee, and trying to decide on my next step. I had spent the entire day in Halifax, going from jewelry store to jewelry store searching for a ring for Amy. I saw dozens, if not hundreds, of beautiful rings. Large diamonds, small ones. Stones so perfect the sparkle was immense. Colored diamonds. Various settings.

And none of them were right.

I had looked over drawings, ideas, and concepts.

Nothing struck a chord.

Nothing said Amy.

I wasn't sure what to do other than perhaps propose without a ring and have Amy choose the one she wanted.

Except I didn't want to do that. When I'd impulsively asked Kelsey to marry me, she immediately showed me the ring she wanted. Large, expensive, and ostentatious—and the only one she would accept. It should have been a warning sign, but I'd bought it for her. It felt as if it was part of a transaction and not a gift of love. I wanted this time to be different.

I leaned my head back, racking my brain. I would search online and see if I found something. Perhaps I could take a picture to one of the jewelers I had spoken with and they could duplicate it.

Someone slid into the booth across from me, and I lifted my head, cracking my eyes open. Holly's amused gaze met mine. "Hey, stranger," she quipped.

I chuckled, having seen her this morning when I'd dropped off Mia. "Hi, yourself."

"What are you doing here?" she asked. "And looking frustrated for? The money world not pleasing you?"

Gladys appeared with a cup of coffee for Holly and refilled my mug. She chatted for a minute, then left. Holly took a sip of her coffee and grimaced. "I will never be a fan of decaf." She rubbed her growing tummy. "But that's the way it has to be right now."

I laughed. "You'll need the caffeine once number four shows up."

She joined in my amusement. "Yep." Then she became serious. "What's up?"

I studied her for a moment and decided to tell her. Maybe she could help.

"What's up is that I have spent hours shopping for an item I cannot seem to locate."

"What sort of item?"

"A ring. For Amy."

She blinked, then her eyes widened and she leaned forward, excited. "A ring? As in engagement?"

"Yes." I ran a hand over my face, feeling the frustration build. I told Holly about my failed trip into Halifax. How I wasn't sure what to do next.

For a moment, she said nothing, then turned and called over to Gladys. "May we have a piece of your blueberry pie? With ice cream. Two forks."

Then she turned back to me. "You know she would love any ring you gave her because it's from you and of what it symbolizes."

"But I want it perfect for her."

The pie came, and she cut off a large bite and took it. She shut her eyes and chewed slowly. I took a bite as well because Gladys's pies were incredible and blueberry was my favorite.

"Why is it you men always do things in the most difficult fashion?"

"Pardon me?"

Holly ate another bite. "Instead of asking her best friend for advice, you spend a day running around Halifax without a clue as to what you are looking for."

"And if I'd asked you first?"

"I would have told you the exact ring Amy would love. Shown it to you right here."

"*What?*"

She grinned. "Let me have the rest of the pie, and I'll show you too."

I snagged one last bite and pushed the plate her way. "Eat fast, Holly."

As she finished the pie, I paid the bill, and together we walked down the street and around the corner to the small antique shop in town. The windows were filled with pieces of bric-a-brac, china, oddities from eras long ago. I had been inside a couple of times—even purchased a great old leather chair for my office here. I was certain the chair Holly had bought for Amy had come from here as well. It was a nice shop, but why we were here, I wasn't sure.

Inside, the owner, Mr. Wilson, came out from around the counter, beaming. "Holly, my dear, how are you?"

"Good," she replied, kissing his cheek.

He shook my hand. "Simon Fletcher," he said after a brief pause. "The burgundy leather club chair."

I grinned. "That's right."

"And the chair and a half. That was for you as well."

"It was," I agreed. "Both are well used."

"Good to hear."

"Is Helen here?" Holly asked.

"Here I am, dear," the woman herself called out,

bustling from the back. She was short, stout, and her white hair was swept up in a bun. Her dark eyes were like raisins in her face, and she had dimples on either side of her smiling mouth. I hadn't met her before, and Holly introduced us. Helen shook my hand firmly.

"Aren't you a handsome one. Replacing Evan, are we?" she teased.

Holly laughed and laid her hand on my arm. "He belongs to Amy."

Helen clapped her hands. "How wonderful." Then her dark eyes widened. "Don't tell me. Really? Amy's ring?"

Holly nodded, looking excited. "Yes."

"I knew it!" She turned and hurried away.

I looked at Holly. "*Amy's* ring?" I repeated.

"Helen purchased a ring at an auction about two years ago. Amy and I were browsing one day, and Helen showed it to us. Amy fell in love with it. She thought it was the most beautiful ring she'd ever seen. She tried it on, and it fit her perfectly."

"I didn't know they had jewelry here. Aside from costume."

"At the back under lock and key. Helen only shows her best pieces to serious buyers. But she knows us and wanted to show it off. She bought it because of how lovely it was and the quality of the workmanship and stones. But given the price point, she's never sold it. Amy always jokes with her and asks how her ring is. Helen always replies she is keeping it safe for her."

Helen appeared, calling us to the back of the store. There was a display case of some nice pieces I hadn't noticed until now. But it was the little leather pouch in Helen's hand that had my interest. She turned on the light beside her and indicated my hand. I held it out, and she dropped a small but surprisingly heavy ring into my palm. I felt a flutter of anticipation as I held it up and looked at it under the light.

It was white gold, with a square-shaped setting, a decent-sized central diamond, surrounded by beautiful blue sapphires. The corners of the square each held another diamond, and smaller ones were woven into the filagree on the band and around the sapphires. They reminded me of the color of Amy's eyes when they were darkened with passion. Rich and intense. The different cuts of diamonds and sapphires used made it exceptional. The ring was beautiful and unique. Like Amy. A one of a kind.

"I had it looked over and the claws fixed. It was cleaned professionally and is in perfect shape. The quality is extraordinary. Circa 1920s."

I looked up. "And she loves it?"

"Very much." Helen slid a piece of paper my way. "Here is the appraisal. I had it redone a few months ago. I was going to put it online to sell in an auction. But I kept putting it off. I think I know why now."

I read the appraisal. The center diamond was a carat. Small by some standards, but with Amy's petite hands and delicate fingers, it would be perfect. The shape and style of the ring suited her. Everything in the appraisal showed the quality. The high color and clarity of the stones used to create it. The beautiful workmanship. I could see it on Amy's finger. I already knew the reaction it would get when I offered it to her.

This was the ring I'd been searching for.

"I'll take it."

"The price—"

I waved my hand. "I'll pay the asking price. This is Amy's ring. I want her to have it."

Holly squealed into her hands. Helen beamed.

"I'll ring it up," she quipped.

I laughed, feeling as if a weight had been lifted off my shoulders. "You do that."

Holly nudged me. "How are you going to ask her?"

"I've got a plan."

"If we can help, let us know."

"I will."

AMY

I finished tidying the classroom and sat at my desk, looking around to make sure everything was in order. The week had gone by at its usual brisk speed. Simon and I kept a careful watch on Mia, but she seemed perfectly normal. No nightmares or worries. No acting out at school. She had a couple other questions for Simon about Kelsey, but more curious than anxious. It seemed the encounter with her mother was something that didn't bother her and she didn't place any significance on. I was grateful for that, and I knew Simon was relieved.

Simon.

I still couldn't believe I had him in my life. He was incredible. A dream lover. A fabulous father. Supportive, loving, and kind. Despite everything he'd gone through with his ex, he was still so open to love.

And he loved me.

I had no doubt. I had never been treated the way he treated me. The envy I'd often felt for Holly when I would watch her and Evan together was long gone, because I had the same thing with Simon.

He'd been busy this week. Quieter than usual, although still affectionate and sweet. I assumed he had something big going with his business since he was on the phone a lot. I was wrapping up the course I was taking, looking forward to it being over. I loved the space I had in the house, but most of the time, I wanted to be downstairs with him and Mia. I enjoyed my time with them and had a sudden dislike of my apartment and being alone. I had to admit, part of me was waiting for him to ask me to move in again. I wanted to. More than I ever expected to want something like that. I wanted to be fully immersed in a life with him and Mia.

A knock on my door made me look up. Eleanor

Aldridge was there, looking uneasy and waiting for me to bade her to enter.

I waved at her. "Come in."

Of all the unexpected things to happen from the Kelsey incident, Eleanor's sudden change of attitude was the biggest shock. She had been horrified at what occurred. Upset that she hadn't seen what Kelsey was doing. Grateful I had walked out of the school when I did.

She had apologized to the principal, to me, and to Simon. She'd even offered her resignation, but Simon had waved her off, shocked at the offer.

"This was Kelsey's fault," he insisted. "She caused all of it. The fire alarm, everything. She wanted you distracted. Let's put it behind us and move forward."

Since then, she had changed. Softened, perhaps. She was still stiff, but I had noticed some laughter come from her classroom. The kids smiled more. She was friendlier and didn't scowl as much.

"Hi, Eleanor," I greeted her.

"Hello, Amy," she replied, coming in and leaning against the table across from my desk. "Looking forward to the weekend?"

"Always."

"Any big plans?"

This was also new—the chatting. But I encouraged it.

"Not really. Mia mentioned a picnic, but it might be too cold. Sunday, my parents are coming out. What about you?"

"Oh, um, nothing really. I need to do some organizing at the apartment. I, ah, don't tend to do a lot of things on the weekends except get ready for the week ahead."

I heard an underlying tone of pain in her voice. A loneliness I hadn't detected until now. An idea hit me, and I decided to go with it. "You know, Holly and I are going shopping next weekend for some craft stuff in Halifax at the fair. The Christmas items are coming in, and we like to plan some fun things for the kids. I always find great ideas for my class as well. Maybe you'd like to come with us?"

Her face paled in shock, and she blinked. "You're asking me to come along? With you and your, ah, friend? Angela's mom?"

"Yes, Holly is Angela's mom, and yes, I am inviting you."

I was shocked to see the glimmer of tears in her eyes. "Really?"

I stood and rounded the desk, standing in front of her. "Yes," I said again. "Really."

"Why?" she asked. "I've been so miserable. Why—"

I cut her off. "Because you're trying. And I think there is more to you than the scowls and sharp words. I know you've been hurt. And frankly, I think you could use a friend. And I also think we could get along well if you would let me in."

She blinked again, processing my words.

"A friend," she murmured. "I haven't had one of

those in a long time." She huffed out a deep sigh. "The last one I had slept with my husband and stole him from me."

My eyes widened at her statement. Then she met my gaze with a shrug. "Not that he was much of a prize, as it turns out. I am better on my own, I think." And she smiled. A real smile. It softened her features, transforming her into a pretty woman. "Still…"

I reached out and rubbed her arm. "That must have devastated you. I can understand it would be hard to trust people, but if you want to try, I would like you to come."

She bit her lip. "Can I–can I think about it?"

"Of course. Let me know."

She swallowed and turned for the door, and I returned to my desk to pick up my things. "Amy," she began, waiting until I looked up from getting my purse.

"Thank you. For being kind. For the offer. After the way I behaved, I really don't deserve it, but I'm grateful. And I think I would like to go."

"Okay. We can talk about it this week. Maybe have lunch one day."

Another smile broke out on her face. "Okay. Have a good weekend."

"You too."

She left, and I picked up my phone, seeing a message from Simon.

SIMON

Simon says hurry home, Chippy. We got pizza and movies.

And my mouth misses yours.

I smiled at the screen and typed a reply.

AMY

On my way.

Amy needs Simon too.

He replied as I walked across the parking lot to my car.

SIMON

Good.

We're waiting.

My footsteps became faster.

Simon frowned after he finished chewing his last bite of pizza. "What do you think has caused this change?"

I sipped my wine, the mellow tones of the red washing over my taste buds. Simon always had good wine on hand. Mia had finished her pizza and was busy arranging our snuggle area for the movie fest. I had told him about the conversation with Eleanor and my impromptu invitation.

"I don't know for sure, but it has something to do with what happened last week. It was as if I proved something to her. What, I have no idea. And I don't know if she will come with us or not. I spoke to Holly, and she was fine with it. She said Eleanor had made a point to say hello to her twice this week, and she noticed that she smiled more at the children." I took another sip of wine. "I think something terrible happened to her, Simon. More than her divorce. Maybe what she needs is a friend or two to help her."

He leaned close, cupping my face. He kissed me. Once. Twice. Three times. "God, I love you," he breathed out. "You are incredible."

"What makes you say that?"

"You could turn your back. Ignore her. Treat her the way she has treated you. Instead, you extend an olive branch."

"I'm just trying to be nice."

"You are still incredible."

"Well, I'm glad you think so."

He sat back, picking up his wine. "Now, about this craft fair you're attending. Evan is gonna have to watch the kids. A client is coming to town to meet with me. He agreed to come here since I was just in Toronto and I'm not willing to go back so soon. He says he is going to bring his wife and make a holiday out of it. So I spoke with Evan, and he is going to keep the kids busy. We'll have supper at their place after. He is planning on a feast. He got a new smoker he is dying to try out."

I chuckled. "It's almost November."

"Doesn't matter. Cook outside, eat inside. It's barbecue, woman."

I had to laugh. He and Evan were crazy for barbecue.

"Sounds good."

"If your day goes well with Eleanor, invite her to dinner."

"Oh, that is a good idea."

He smiled and leaned close again, capturing my mouth. This time, the kiss was deeper. Hotter. Wetter. He cupped the back of my head, angling his to get closer. He hummed in satisfaction as our tongues stroked together. I sighed, slipping my arms around his neck, losing myself to the taste and feel of him.

Until Mia ran in, sliding in front of us.

"You're kissing again?"

We broke apart, both of us smiling.

"Amy had something in her eye," Simon fibbed. "I was looking really closely."

"Daddy," she admonished, shaking her head in vexation. "I'm not a baby. I know what kissing looks like."

He grinned, not at all ashamed of being caught. "Blankets ready?"

"Yes. But you hafta get in your jammies," she insisted.

I headed for the stairs. "That sounds amazing. I'm looking forward to this."

"I picked the movies!" Mia exclaimed.

"I bet Dory is in the lineup," Simon muttered behind me on the stairs. "At least she'll be so busy watching, she won't see us making out."

"In your dreams," I replied. "She'll be between us."

He chuckled. "Let's hope she falls asleep fast."

I glanced over my shoulder. "Can't you just behave for a couple of hours?"

He grabbed me at the top of the landing, spinning me around and kissing me again. "If I have to. Unless, of course, you need help getting into your jammies. Or out of them." He nipped my neck. "I hear the movie starting. She'll be distracted, and we could be fast."

I pushed him away, laughing, refusing to allow him to see how tempted I was. One of us had to be responsible.

"I will meet you downstairs," I said, grabbing my pajamas. "Fully clothed and untouched."

"Fine," he grumped good-naturedly. "But you'll have to make up for it later."

"Whatever, Fletcher," I called over my shoulder. I planned to enjoy the movie and popcorn first.

But later was certainly going to be fun.

CHAPTER NINETEEN

SIMON

After the movie fest, the popcorn, and Mia's excited chatter, pointing out all the things she didn't want us to miss in her favorite movies, she finally fell asleep. A handful of popcorn was still clutched in her fist, *Frozen* was still playing, but she had eventually worn herself out. I carried her upstairs, tucking her in and kissing her forehead.

I returned downstairs, sitting beside Amy, who was drowsy and content in the corner of the sofa, still half watching the movie.

"She all tucked in?"

"Yeah." I chuckled. "Looks like I'll be doing the same thing for you soon."

She smiled. "Nah, I'll get my second wind."

I kissed her. "Good."

"She was wound up tonight. Excited. I wonder why?" Amy mused.

I knew exactly why but kept that to myself.

"Good week at school. Oh, and she got another sleepover invite."

Amy smiled. "She's settled in so well."

I sat back, linking our hands. "We both have. But yeah, she is happy here. She has more friends than she did in Ontario. She never really fit it in there. I suppose neither of us did."

"You fit in here very well."

I leaned over and kissed her again. "I fit with you really well." I grinned as I grasped her around the waist, tugging her to my lap, and she gasped. "Feel how well we fit?"

She wound her arms around my neck, widening her legs and straddling me. Even with the material between us, I felt her heat. "I love how you fit me," she whispered against my mouth.

I had no idea what it was about this woman. My cock acted as if he was twenty whenever she was around. He couldn't get enough. I couldn't get enough. I had never experienced passion the way I did with her. As soon as she was close, I wanted her closer. I wanted to feel her skin on mine, her taste in my mouth, her hands on me.

I pulled her tight to my chest and kissed her. She tasted of wine and salty popcorn. Sweetness underlined the taste from the jujubes she'd nibbled on. She tasted like Amy. It was highly addictive. As our tongues stroked together, she made that noise. My favorite one. A low whimper combined with a sigh I felt deep in my bones. It told me how strongly affected she was—the fact that she wanted me as much as I wanted her.

We moved together as we kissed endlessly, the friction and delayed gratification slow and delicious. I loved how she felt riding me—sliding along my hardness, the promise of what was to come intense and thrilling.

"Take me upstairs, Simon," she begged.

"I want to see you come first," I murmured, sliding my hand into her waistband. "Ride my fingers, Chippy. Take the edge off. Then I'll take you upstairs and fuck you until you scream."

She whimpered again as I played with her. Teased her stiff nub, circled her where I knew she was aching and wanting to be filled. She dropped her head to my shoulder, turning her face to my neck, her hot breath washing over my skin. She curled her hand around the material of my T-shirt, my name falling from her lips. "Simon, oh God, Simon."

"Give it to me," I demanded, knowing she loved it when I was vocal and bossy, as she put it. I slid two fingers inside her, pumping hard. "Come on my hand."

She stiffened, burying her face in my neck as she cried out softly. I worked her until she collapsed against me heavily, her breathing ragged.

I kissed the top of her head, withdrawing my fingers and licking them. She watched me, her eyes wide, the desire not yet gone. I met her gaze with a grin. "Round one, baby. Round two upstairs where—"

She interrupted me, sliding off my lap. "Round two is right here." She grabbed my waistband, tugging. "Right now."

My cock sprang free, and she engulfed it in her mouth. I groaned low and heavy in my chest. I hadn't planned on that, but I was more than happy to accommodate. Amy between my knees with my cock filling her mouth was always an acceptable addition to the plan.

Any plan.

Early the next morning, I slid from bed, leaving Amy sleeping. Round two had morphed into rounds three and four in the night, and she was exhausted. I was too keyed up to rest. I had a lot of things to make happen before she woke up. I showered and pulled on clean clothes, casting one last look at her asleep in our bed. Her wild curls were spread around the pillow, and she was burrowed under the quilt, clutching my pillow close to her body. One leg stuck out the bottom, the slender calf pale against the dark cinnamon of the material.

Even asleep, she enticed me.

I backed out of the door, shutting it behind me. I checked on Mia, seeing she was okay, then headed downstairs.

I made the pancake batter and slid the bacon into the oven to cook, then headed to the family room, moving a few things around and using the blankets from last night to make a picnic area in front of the fireplace. It was dark and gloomy outside, which was a perfect excuse for a fire and the candles on the mantel to be lit. I made sure everything was in place and headed back to the kitchen, smiling at the sound of little feet thumping down the steps and heading my way. I turned and held out my arms for Mia. She flung herself into my embrace, her eyes glowing with excitement. "Today, Daddy?"

"Yeah, Sweet Pea. Today."

"I can help!"

"Yes, you can. We're gonna make the pancakes small so we can eat them easier. You can help me pour and flip them."

She pursed her lips. "We still get peanut butter and syrup, right?"

I chuckled in amusement. Amy had gotten her on to that combination. I had to admit, it wasn't bad, but I preferred lots of butter and jam on mine. "Yes."

She slid down. "Okay, Daddy. Let's do it!"

We worked quickly, making the pancakes, taking the bacon from the oven. We scattered some flowers I had been hiding overnight in the living room and lit the candles, giving the room a pretty look. When I heard the shower come on, I knew Amy would be down soon. I wanted this morning to go well. I wasn't worried about Amy's response to my question, but I was oddly nervous. It felt like the most important thing I had ever done. Maybe because, to me, she was the key to the happiness I had discovered. I didn't want to ever lose that. Plus, I wanted this morning to be special.

I had planned and dismissed a hundred ideas on how to ask Amy to marry me. Researched places, scanned websites, even spoken to companies that helped you create the perfect scenario. Except, like the ring, none of them felt right. They were too much, too over the top. Too fake and contrived.

Until I really thought about it. It was Amy. I didn't have to prove my love to her, and she would want something simple. Something that embodied *us*. And most importantly, included Mia.

So, I planned a special breakfast for her. All her favorites with one addition.

A question and a ring.

And it was time to put that idea into play.

I heard her footsteps on the stairs, and I peered down at Mia. "Ready, Sweet Pea?"

Her eyes were large and excited. "Yeah."

"You only have to keep it secret a little longer."

"I can do it, Daddy."

I bent and kissed her. "I know you can."

Then I turned to the stove. "Act natural."

Mia giggled, and I knew why. Of the two of us, I was going to be the one to mess this up.

Of that, I had no doubt.

AMY

I headed downstairs, the scent of coffee and bacon in the air. I loved waking up to breakfast with Simon and Mia. It was sort of our thing. From the first morning when Simon was trying to smuggle me out of the house and Mia appeared, announcing pancakes were for fun sleepovers, we had made it part of our routine. Simon and Mia always got up and made it together.

Waking up in Simon's bed was still new and addictive. The scent of him surrounded me. The recollection of what we had done the night before was still fresh in my mind. He'd been relentless, wringing one orgasm after another from me. He was wound up about something, and I would have to figure out what it was.

I wasn't sure I would be able to walk after another marathon session like last night.

But I had to admit, I couldn't stop smiling.

My smile grew bigger as I walked into the kitchen. My two favorite people were at the stove, the scent of pancakes adding to the already delicious aromas. "Morning," I called out.

I was greeted with two smiles. "Hey, Chippy," Simon said with a wink. "How'd you sleep?"

I felt my blush. He knew how I'd slept. Thanks to his sexual appetite, I was exhausted.

"Good, thanks."

Mia climbed off the chair and ran over, flinging her arms around my legs. "We're having a breakfast picnic."

"Oh?" I asked.

Simon nodded, flipping the pancakes. "Cold and wet outside, so we thought we'd have an early picnic instead today."

"Good plan."

He handed me a cup of coffee, kissing me quickly. "Go sit, and we'll bring it in."

"I can help," I protested.

"Nope. We got this. Right, Sweet Pea?"

Mia nodded her head vigorously. "Yep."

I walked into the living area, gasping at the setup. The fire was on, casting a warmth into the room. Candles flickered, adding a glow that banished the dull light from outside. Warm blankets were on the floor, and flowers were scattered around as if we were outside. In the middle of the blanket was a small vase with more flowers, and there were even pillows to rest on. It was lovely and thoughtful.

I sat down, cross-legged, shaking my head in wonder. Whatever possessed Simon to do this I had no idea, but I loved it. An indoor picnic while outside it rained and stormed. He was ingenious.

He came in, carrying a tray. It held plates of small pancakes and bacon. Bowls of syrup and jam. Butter. Peanut butter. Mia had smaller plates, napkins, and utensils.

They set everything up, and Simon disappeared,

coming back with juice for Mia and a carafe of coffee. I exclaimed over everything, and we began to eat.

We laughed as we discarded the forks, instead spreading on the peanut butter and dipping the little pancakes in the syrup. Simon preferred them with butter and syrup or jam, but Mia and I liked my combination the best. We ate bacon with our fingers, licking off the grease. Simon went and got some wet towels for us to clean up with, but the stickiness and grease were part of the fun. I noticed he was a little tense, and I wondered why but put off asking until we were alone later. Still, he laughed and teased Mia, made sure she ate and drank her juice and didn't spill more than she consumed. She seemed overly excited, but I put it down to the picnic and the sugar.

Finally, we were done eating and had piled the dishes onto the tray, the pancakes and bacon still between us for snacking. I wiped my fingers and picked up my coffee, meeting Simon's gaze.

"That was amazing. Thank you."

He nodded, looking somber. I sat straighter. "Simon? What is it?"

He looked at Mia and cleared his throat.

"Amy, you came into our life and changed it. I'm not sure you realize how much."

I blinked in surprise at the sudden shift in atmosphere. It felt serious.

"Oh," was all I said.

"You became a partner, a friend…" He smiled. "My best friend. A surrogate mom for Mia."

"I love you both," I replied, my heart beginning to beat faster.

"We love you."

Mia scooted next to Simon, who smiled and wrapped his arm around her. She was almost vibrating now in anticipation, and I felt my eyes fill with tears at his next words.

"We wanted to know if you would do us the honor of becoming my wife. Mia's mom. Making us a family." He held out a small leather pouch. "If you would accept this as a token of how much you are loved. How much you would be loved for the rest of your life."

I covered my mouth with my hand. He wanted to love me for the rest of my life. They wanted me to belong to them. They already belonged to me.

A sob burst from my mouth, and all I could do was nod. "Y-yes," I managed to get out through my lips.

In a blur of motion, I was in his arms. Mia was there too, and we were hugging. Laughing. Crying. He held me tight, whispering his love and his promises of forever. Kissing me. Mia kissing me. Me kissing them both. Holding Mia's sweet face between my hands and knowing this was where I belonged. Seeing the glow of love in Simon's warm hazel eyes I would never grow tired of witnessing.

He pulled back and grimaced. "I knew I would mess something up."

I looked down and began to laugh. His knee was

squarely in the plate of pancakes, the bowl of syrup knocked over and soaking into his pants. I threw my arms back around his neck. "You didn't mess anything up. It's perfect. It's all perfect."

He kissed me. "You're the perfect one. Perfect for us. Now open your ring so I can go change my pants."

I didn't think I could fall in love with him more. But as I opened the pouch with my shaky fingers and saw the ring—the one I had fallen in love with so long ago—it happened.

I looked up, fresh tears in my eyes. "How?" I whispered.

He took the ring from me, sliding it on my finger. The diamonds glittered even in the muted lighting, and the sapphires shimmered a brilliant blue with them. "Holly," he said.

"It's so pretty!" Mia exclaimed.

"It's the most beautiful ring in the world," I murmured, staring at it.

"For the most beautiful woman in the world."

There was no doubting the sincerity in his voice. He truly believed that. To him, I *was* the most beautiful woman. That was how he saw me. That was how the love he felt for me made him see me.

"Amy," Simon said, his voice serious once again.

I glanced up.

"Soon, okay? I want to marry you soon. I asked your parents, they gave me their blessing, so we need to plan and do this soon. Whatever you want, however you want it, all I ask is for it to happen soon. I want our life together to start now."

And for the second time that morning, I began to cry.

"Yes."

CHAPTER TWENTY

SIMON

Pancake- and syrup-free, I headed back down the stairs toward the kitchen. Mia was in her room, talking excitedly to her dolls and stuffed animals about her new mommy. Before I'd gone upstairs to change, we'd quickly cleaned off the blankets and took the dishes to the kitchen. I wasn't surprised to find Amy sitting at the island in the kitchen with fresh coffee brewing.

I stopped in the doorway, studying her. She stared at her ring, tracing the stones with the tip of a finger, her wild curls hiding her face. I wondered what she was thinking. Was she contemplating the wedding? Our life together? The changes that would happen? My odd proposal?

I stole up behind her, looping my arms around her waist and tugging her back to my chest. She sighed as I brushed her hair away from her shoulder, settling my chin there and turning my head to press a kiss to her cheek.

"You really like it, Chippy?"

"If I could have any ring in the entire world, I would pick this one."

I tightened my arms. "Good. I searched for an entire day. I looked at every kind of ring the jewelry stores in Halifax had to offer. At custom sites on the web. I was considering flying to Toronto to look when Holly found me and took me to see this one." I held up her hand and kissed her fingers. "It's unique and beautiful. Like you."

"You really believe that," she whispered, the wonder in her voice evident.

I spun her around on the stool and braced my arms on the island, trapping her between them. "Yes. I believe it because you are."

She cupped my face. "Thank you."

"So we get a license this week and get married the day we pick it up?" I asked hopefully.

She laughed. "If that's what you want."

"What do *you* want?" I already knew because both Holly and her mom had told me, but I wanted to hear it from her.

"I always wanted to get married by the water. My family and a few friends. Some pretty flowers. A nice dinner." She smiled and touched my cheek. "To dance with my new husband."

I smiled at her words. The last part hadn't been mentioned to me, but I liked the idea of dancing with

Amy—as her husband. I drew in a long breath before I spoke.

"We could get married at Edgewater. I checked with Alex, and she said she could arrange it for us. The private dining room that overlooks the ocean. We could do it all there if you wanted. Get married with the ocean behind us. Host a weekend. Have the cottage again and have the family stay at the hotel. Get some pictures outside as long as it's not too cold."

She blinked, her eyes filling with tears. "Really?"

"Can you find a dress in three weeks?" I asked.

"Three weeks?"

"Alex might have blocked some space for me, as a favor. I told her I would let her know today."

Amy was quiet, a thousand emotions flitting across her face. I knew I was moving fast, but I had meant what I said earlier. I wanted our life together to start now. If she needed more time, I understood and I would convince her to move in with us, but I really wanted to marry her soon.

"Simon," she whispered.

I braced myself for her gentle refusal.

"Yeah, Chippy?"

"Three weeks is doable. Make that call."

I yanked her to my chest and kissed her. I poured all the love, joy, and excitement I was feeling into that kiss. She returned my enthusiasm, holding me tight, our tongues sliding together. I vaguely heard the phone ringing and the sound of Mia's voice somewhere close.

"They're kissing again, Auntie Holly. If I ask, Daddy will say something silly about Amy's eyes, so I won't ask. Do you and Uncle E kiss all the time?"

I pulled back, meeting Amy's amused eyes. "Busted again." I kissed her one more time, unable to resist. "Welcome to your new life."

"I look forward to it."

"Me too."

Later that afternoon, Evan grinned at me over the rim of his coffee cup.

"Three weeks?"

"Yep. Alex has the place booked. I got rooms and cabins for everyone. We already filed the application for the license." I glanced toward the sofa where the girls were gathered, laughing and talking. "Holly and Amy can handle the dresses. Alex will help with the flowers. I booked the justice of the peace and the photographer."

"You were prepared."

"I worked all week on the details in case she agreed."

"You really had doubts?"

"About her marrying me? No. But doing this quickly, yes. I was hopeful, though."

"She loves you."

I grinned at him. "I know. This time, it's for all the

right reasons." I picked up my coffee. "Will you stand up with me, Evan?"

He paused, then smiled. "Absolutely. It would be my honor."

"Amy is asking Holly. The only other person in the wedding party is Mia."

"She'll love it."

Across the room, Holly squealed and hugged Amy, so I knew the question had been asked. Everything was coming together well. In three weeks, Amy would be my wife, and our life would start.

We would find our way together.

And I was looking forward to that.

AMY

The light caught my ring, capturing my attention. I'd never been much for expensive jewelry, but this piece made my heart flutter. Not only because of the reason I wore it, but simply due to the fact that it was a tiny work of art on my hand. In the week that had passed since Simon had asked me to marry him, we had been busy arranging plans for the wedding. Even as simple as we were going, there were a lot of details. My parents were thrilled, my mother exclaiming in delight as I showed her around the house I would soon be permanently calling my home. She told me how much my dad loved the fact that Simon had gone into Halifax on his own to ask for their blessing. How he had assured them he would look after me and make sure I never wanted for anything and it was his goal to make me happy. *We were thrilled to give him our blessing,* she enthused. *Such a wonderful man.*

Add in the fact that she adored Mia, and thrilled didn't cover it.

"What do you think is taking Eleanor so long?" Holly asked, her concerned voice bringing me out of my musings.

"I'm not sure. I texted to let her know we were here."

A text popped up that made me frown. "She says something came up. That we should go without her."

Holly grimaced. "I don't think so. You said she was nervous about coming with us. She's overreacting. Let's go get her."

We headed to the building, walking in with another tenant and knocking on Eleanor's door. She answered, looking frazzled and upset. She gaped when she saw it was us.

"I can't go. Didn't you get my text?"

Holly walked past her. "Yes."

I followed her. "We didn't believe you."

She looked flabbergasted. "What?"

"What is it?" I asked. "Your nerves? The thought of spending the afternoon with us?" I leaned forward, dropping my voice. "Because Holly is beginning to waddle like a penguin? You can pretend she isn't. We all do."

Eleanor's lips quirked. Holly began to laugh in protest. "I am not waddling yet. It's too soon."

I winked at Eleanor. "Uh-huh. Okay, Holly."

I became serious. "Why won't you come?"

"I have nothing to wear. My hair is just so…awful. And I'm too nervous," she burst out.

"You don't have to be nervous. And we can help. We'll have you ready in five minutes. Right, Holly?"

"If I can waddle that fast," she replied dryly.

This time, Eleanor did laugh. She drew in a deep breath and nodded. "Okay. I'll go."

Three hours later, we sat down at the café in the large auditorium. I groaned as I rotated my shoulders. "I am done. I can't believe how much stuff I got."

Holly grinned. "I told you to bring a rolling tote bag along. Evan wouldn't let me come unless I had it with me."

Eleanor came over, bringing the tray. She sat down, handing us our coffees. I barely recognized her. We had brushed out her hair, and I was shocked how long it was, hanging down her back and past her waist. It showed off the slightly reddish tinge to her light brown tresses, and it suited her. I'd pulled a sweater from her closet she had obviously never worn and added it to the jeans she was wearing. Holly found a pretty floral shirt we handed her, and I discovered a pair of ankle boots still in the box and made her put them on.

She'd looked apprehensive but allowed us to treat her like a Barbie doll. She had rolled her eyes when we assured her she looked great and was obviously uncomfortable at first. But once we were at the craft fair, she forgot about everything but the fair and was as into it as we were.

I thanked her for the coffee, and she smiled. "Put that hand down. You're blinding me."

I laughed. She had been cordial and congratulated me at work on Monday when she saw the ring, exclaiming over the beauty of it. It surprised me, but I was pleased.

"Have you made your plans?" she asked.

"Everything is all set. It's going to be very simple. My parents and my brother, some friends. A quick ceremony, pretty flowers, a nice dinner, cake, and dancing. No gifts, no fuss."

"A party, really," she surmised.

"Yes, I suppose. I want a lovely day with the people I care about. I want pictures to look back on. I don't want to be stressing that someone's shoes don't match mine."

They laughed.

Eleanor took a sip of her coffee. "What about a dress?"

"That's my biggest issue. I am wearing my mom's. She brought it with her last week. I need it altered, but Mrs. Gallagher at the Sewing Center hurt her wrist and she can't do it now."

Holly grimaced. "I don't know anyone else. I can stitch a broken seam, but that's about it."

"What has to be done?" Eleanor asked.

"Nothing major. A tuck or two in the waist and tightening the shoulders, a torn hem, and a few pieces of lace to be repaired. But sewing is not my forte. Mrs. Gallagher was going to call a few friends to see if they could fit it in."

"I can do it," Eleanor offered.

"What?"

"I love to sew. I make quilts and a lot of my own clothes. I can alter the dress for you."

Reaching over, I clasped her hand. "Really?"

"Yes, of course." She paused. "That's what friends are for, right? To help one another?"

I beamed at her. "Yes."

On the way home, I shared a look with Holly, who turned to Eleanor in the back seat. "We would like it if you came for supper with us at our place."

Eleanor looked surprised. "Really?"

"Yes."

"Oh, ah…"

"We can stop by my apartment, and you can look at the dress, then we'll go to Holly's place. I'll drive you home later," I offered. "Please."

"I'd like that."

"Great."

At the apartment, I put on my mom's dress, and Eleanor studied me. "Do you have pins?"

I laughed and handed her a box. "Mom brought these with her."

Eleanor tugged and smoothed, pinned and adjusted, then stepped back. "There," she said, taking a few pins from between her lips. "That's better."

I looked in the mirror. The tea-length dress was a rich cream with a nipped-in waist and a full skirt. The top was strapless, but the whole dress was overlaid in lace. The covering ended at my elbows and had an intricate scallop around the neck. A thin belt wrapped around the waist. I fingered a piece of the torn lace. "Can this be fixed?"

"Absolutely."

Holly clapped her hands. "It's perfect for you. Simon is going to love it."

"Mia picked a blue dress online this week, and it came last night. Fits her like a dream. She loved it—especially the sparkles."

Holly grinned. "I got my dress too. Empire waist in case baby in here grows even more than I expect."

I took Eleanor's hand. "Will you come to the wedding?"

"Oh, I can't."

"Please. You can make sure the dress is okay and enjoy the day. It's small, so no need to be nervous."

"I won't know anyone…" She trailed off.

"You can sit with us," Holly said.

"And my parents. My brother. Sheldon won't know anyone either. Please come."

A pleased smile crossed her face. "Okay."

"Perfect."

SIMON

I woke up, putting my hand out for Amy, only to find cold sheets. I sat up, looking around. The door to the bathroom was open, but the one to the hall was shut. I pushed back the blankets and grabbed my sweats, tugging them on. I wandered down the hall toward her office, seeing the sliver of light coming out from under the door.

I twisted the door handle and went into the room. Amy was at her desk, a book open in front of her. She was making an entry, looking up startled as I walked in.

"Hi," she mumbled, closing the book.

"What are you doing?"

"Wedding stuff."

"At two in the morning?"

"I couldn't sleep, so I thought I would do a few things."

I sat in the chair. "Couldn't sleep?" I questioned.

"I had far too much coffee today with Eleanor and Holly. Plus two cups of Evan's java after dinner. I'm still wired."

I chuckled. "I barely recognized Eleanor when you brought her into the house. Talk about a transformation."

"She's so pretty," Amy said, drawing her knees up to her chest. "And lost. She is funny and smart. But so afraid to be herself. I'm not sure she knows who

Eleanor is. Under all that snark and attitude, she is really very sweet. I like her."

"Maybe she just needed a friend or two," I stated. "You and Holly will be good for her. And I agree. She was quiet at dinner, but when she spoke, she was funny at times."

Amy nodded, her gaze falling to the book on her desk. I narrowed my eyes, seeing the small title on the cover.

Budget.

I sat back, looking at her. "What are you doing, Chippy? I mean, *really* doing."

"Just keeping track of wedding expenses, my expenses—" She stopped speaking, shrugging. "Making sure I don't overextend."

I realized a conversation needed to happen. We had been so busy planning the future and our lives together, I hadn't sat with Amy and talked this all out. I was awake now, and it was a good time to clear the air.

I sat back, crossing my ankle over my knee. "I have told you that I'm paying for all the wedding expenses, Amy."

"That doesn't seem—"

I cut her off. "As I told your parents, that is my gift to you. To me as well since I'm so damn anxious to marry you."

"I still need to track—"

Again, I stopped her. "Do what you have to do, but there is no budget, Amy. Whatever you want, I want you to have. No scrimping because lilies are more expensive than carnations. Or if there is an overnight shipping charge on an item. Whatever you want to make it the day of your dreams. I want you to have it. Do you understand?"

"I could break you," she said. "I have expensive tastes."

I laughed at her. "No. My ex had expensive taste. You have an eye for lovely things *and* common sense. That's a vast difference. You can't break me, Amy."

She huffed a sigh. "I know you're well-off, Simon. But I will be contributing to this household. Once I sublet the apartment, I'll pay part of the mortgage and the bills…"

"There is no mortgage. I'll cover the apartment rent until you find a subletter because, once again, you're moving fast because of my timeline. As for the bills, we'll figure it out." I stood and went to her desk, picking up her laptop. I typed on the keyboard, then set it back on her desk. "Look."

She turned and looked at the screen. Her posture stiffened and she lifted her head as she realized what she was looking at. I leaned over and rested my chin on her shoulder, seeing the financial picture she was staring at.

"I am more than well-off, Amy. You will never want for anything. If you didn't want to work, you wouldn't have to. My greatest joy in life is going to be looking after you. I want to give you everything—if you let me."

"I-I didn't know," she whispered, shock making her voice raspy. "I don't know if I've seen that many zeros on a bank statement."

I chuckled and pressed a kiss to her neck. "What is mine is yours. That's how marriage works."

"I should sign a prenup."

"Nope. I don't need a prenup with you. I know you, Amy. I trust you more than anyone else in my life. If you decided to leave me, you might as well take it all anyway."

She turned in her chair and glared up at me. "I am not marrying you for your money. I don't care about it. I love you. You and your heart. Not your bank account."

I rested my hands on the arms of her chair, hovering over her. "I know. That's one reason I love you so much. You love me. Just Simon."

"I do."

I grinned. "Keep practicing those words, baby. You'll be saying them in front of a bunch of people soon."

Tears glimmered in her eyes, and I wiped them away. "Please don't worry about the money. A budget for our day. The apartment. Anything. I've got you."

"If what is yours is mine, then what is mine is yours."

I loved her independence. Her determination to be able to look after herself. And her resolve to be an equal partner. I wanted her to relax once we were married and realize how happy it would make me to look after her. She looked after me as well, but in a different way. Her contribution was far more important, and I hoped one day she would see that. Until then, I would keep reminding her.

"I agree. So, can I have your car?" I teased.

She widened her eyes. "My eight-year-old Kia with the rust on it? No way, you gold digger. Hands off the vehicle."

I laughed and bent to kiss her. "My evil plan has been foiled."

She cupped my face. "I love you, Simon."

"I know. I love you right back."

"Can you close that screen now? It makes me jittery."

I logged out and shut the lid. "Come back to bed, and I'll calm your jitters. I have just the thing."

She smiled as I held out my hand. She took it and squeezed my fingers. "I bet you do."

CHAPTER TWENTY-ONE

SIMON

The day I married Kelsey, my stomach had ached from the repressed anxiety I felt. There was no sense of ultimate happiness, no joy. It was a step in a journey I wasn't sure I wanted to be on any longer, yet I felt as if I had no choice but to keep going forward.

The excess and over-the-top day gave me a headache. Kelsey's constant griping about the things she didn't like was endless. Thinking back to the fake smiles on both of our faces in the photos made me shudder.

Today, I woke up excited, hopeful, filled with a sense of purpose. Today, I would marry Amy. Mia would have a mother who loved her. I would have a wife who wanted me for me. Loved me for me. Wanted to build a forever life with me.

Today was going to be an amazing day.

The cabin felt empty. I had spent the night alone,

Mia with Amy up at the main resort with her mother, Holly, and the girls. Amy wanted to observe the last night apart custom and wanted to stay in the main lodge with them. I hated the idea of being without her but agreed. I wasn't sure our late-night phone sex was considered customary, but I enjoyed it. My little Chippy had a lot of pent-up energy she needed relieved. I slept far better than I expected once we hung up.

After the wedding, we would come back to this cabin she loved so much and spend four days alone. Mia was going back to the house with Amy's parents, who would take care of her while we had a brief honeymoon. I planned a longer one for next summer, and Amy had asked if we could go away as a family over spring break. I was only too happy to grant such an unselfish request.

I glanced at the clock with a groan. It was only nine, and the ceremony wasn't until six. Luckily, Evan was coming over to take me to town for breakfast and some bonding time. We could walk around the town and burn off some of this nervous energy. I had been told not to come to the main building until an hour before the service. I didn't dare defy Alex.

When the knock on the door finally sounded, I was pleased to see not only Evan, but Sheldon and Dylan as well.

"Many hands make light work?" I quipped.

"I don't want to know what your hands have been doing. Holly said she heard Amy on the phone late into the night and she wasn't only talking," Evan said with a wide grin as he went past me.

"Oh God, that is my sister," Sheldon groaned.

I laughed. "Never mind your sister. What were you doing trading spit in a dark hallway with Eleanor?"

Evan gaped. "Eleanor?"

Sheldon smirked. "I call her Ellie. It confounds her. She is lovely. Just fucking lovely."

His words and the tone he used surprised me, and I recalled when Eleanor had shown up the previous afternoon.

She walked into the large reception area, wearing a green coat, snowflakes in her burnished hair. The unexpected storm had slowed everyone down, and she was the last to arrive. Amy heaved a sigh of relief, worried over the weather and a last-minute case of nerves on Eleanor's part. She was still hesitant around us, although when she relaxed, she was great company. When I gently suggested that perhaps Amy should not have tasked Eleanor with bringing her dress, Amy rolled her eyes.

"Eleanor prides herself on completing a job. Getting me the dress will override the nerves. That way, I know she will come."

On my other side, Sheldon breathed out a long whistle. "Who is that gorgeous woman?"

I had to admit, Amy and Holly had transformed Eleanor. I wasn't sure about gorgeous, but she was pretty. She wore her hair down more, ditched the drab clothing, and smiled a lot. And today, with a flush on her face, the snow in her hair, and a beaming expression, she was captivating. Sheldon certainly seemed fascinated. Eleanor looked around, spotted Amy and waved. Then she looked toward Sheldon and froze for a moment, unblinking and still. She seemed to have recovered, but she blushed when Amy introduced her to Sheldon. Every time I saw her for the rest of the evening, Sheldon was close. The clinch I caught them in later that night was anything but casual. I had a feeling if I hadn't intruded, that hallway would have been used for things it was not intended by the architect.

Bringing myself back to the present, I met his gaze. "*Lovely*, is she? Exactly how well did you get to know her last night?"

He shook his head. "A gentleman never tells."

That said everything.

"Careful," I said, feeling protective of the woman my soon-to-be wife had become so fond of. "She's not to be trifled with. Amy will skin you alive."

"I have no plans for trifling with her," Sheldon informed me. "I think she is amazing. She seems to like me, so I'm going to get to know her."

"In the biblical way?"

He narrowed his eyes, and Dylan laughed, interrupting us. "Okay, enough grilling. We've got a squash court booked so I can sweat out some of your nerves. Then I have us a pub lunch planned and appointments at the barber. Trims, shaves, whatever you want." He clapped me on the shoulder. "I promised your bride you would look good, and I always keep my promises."

My bride. I liked the sound of that.

I grinned. "Let's go."

Candles flickered, their glow casting shimmers on the glass of the large windows. I waited impatiently, wanting the service to start. Anxious to see my bride. See her smile. Watch the expression on my daughter's face while she walked in front of Amy. Today was a joyous day for all of us.

The room was filled with flowers and candles, the scent of them lingering in the air. I stood at the arbor, my hands linked in front of me, watching the closed double doors, knowing when they opened, my life would change forever.

It was all I could do not to rush down the short aisle and open the doors myself.

I met the gazes of the people waiting with me. Amy's mom, wiping away a tear already. I knew her dad was emotional as well. Her brother Sheldon sat beside his mother, smiling, holding her hand in comfort. He cast his gaze over his shoulder, staring at another guest seated a couple of rows back. I tried not to grin. It would appear Eleanor still had his attention. Every time I glanced over, he was staring in her direction. She seemed to be looking anywhere but toward him.

Interesting.

There were smiles, winks, and thumbs-up from our friends. We only had thirty guests, aside from our families. It was the perfect size.

The justice of the peace tapped my shoulder. "It's time."

"Finally," I muttered, facing the doors as they opened.

Evan and Holly came first, smiling and walking toward me. I got a kiss on the cheek from her and a shoulder clap from Evan, then they took their places. Mia appeared, and the tears started in my eyes. My little girl was in a frilly, sparkly blue dress she had chosen. The flat shoes on her little feet sparkled as well. She walked slowly, scattering blossoms as she went. Her smile was wide, and I bent to kiss her as she stopped in front of me. "Hi, Daddy."

"Hey, Sweet Pea. Good job."

"Wait until you see Mommy. She's so beautiful."

The "Mommy" had started the day we got engaged. The first time Mia used it, Amy cried. She still did at times. I had to admit, I still got choked up on occasion when I heard it.

The music swelled, and Amy appeared on the arm of her father. The sight of her took my breath away. The old-fashioned dress was perfect for her, showing off her curves and slender, shapely legs, the lace on the bodice and arms somehow sexier than if her skin had been bare. Her wild curls were swept away from her face in a fancy updo, a few unruly tendrils hanging around her ears. A sexy little wisp of tulle and lace acted as a headpiece of sorts, and pearls and shimmery beads were nestled in the strands. Diamond studs I had sent her earlier as a wedding gift glimmered in her ears. I watched her approach me, our eyes locked the entire time. I was unable to look away, not wanting to waste one second staring anywhere else. She was my light. My force. My strength. Her love and goodness shone around her.

And she was mine.

I shook her father's hand and enfolded my hand around her palm, pulling her closer.

"I've got her, sir."

He nodded and took his seat. I stared down at her, transfixed by her beauty. She didn't rush me or try to get me to stop. I had to lean down and kiss her. "You are exquisite. Thank you for marrying me today."

She smiled and kissed me back. "You're welcome."

"Ready?"

"Let's do this."

I held Amy close, enjoying dancing with my wife. She fit so well into my arms, her head the perfect height under my chin.

I traced the lace on her back, smiling at the shivers I felt running down her spine. "You almost ready to stop being social and come back to the cabin with me?" I asked. "You've danced with everyone, talked, and smiled. And laughed."

"I ate too."

"Yes, you did. They've had you long enough. I want my wife alone."

Amy tilted up her head, smiling. "Your wife. I like the sound of that."

"I like you."

"I hope so."

"The cabin," I said again. "Come to the cabin with me, and I'll show you how much I like you. I want to peel you out of that sexy dress and see how it looks on the floor."

She laughed softly. "One-track mind."

"For you—yes."

"Have I mentioned how incredible you look in your tux?"

"A few times. Play your cards right, and I'll let you take it off soon."

She scoffed, rolling her eyes. "As if there were any doubt."

Chuckling, I pulled her closer. "Let's go, baby. I want you."

She looked around. "Everyone had a good time. Do you think they'll mind if we leave?"

"They won't even notice. It's already almost eleven, and I've been patient long enough. The kids are asleep. The adults can keep having a good time. It's an open bar, and more food is coming soon. They can eat and drink and pass out in their rooms. No one is driving."

"Oh, the late-night snacks," she said wistfully. "I forgot about those."

I had to smile. "The kitchen is sending us an assortment. I got you, Chippy."

"You got me forever."

I pulled her into my arms and kissed her. Passionately. Not caring who was watching, because now she was entirely mine.

"Exactly what I wanted."

"Then take me to the cabin, husband. Make me yours."

Her words and the feel of her in my arms were perfect.

"Let's go, Mrs. Fletcher. Let's go."

EPILOGUE

SIMON

TWO YEARS LATER

I glanced out the window at the winter wonderland around us. The storm was still blowing, the snow swirling and dense, glittering in the late-afternoon light. Soon, it would be dark, and the snow was forecast to continue to fall. My family was safe and snug in our home, the scent of dinner cooking. Mia and I had made lasagna, still one of our favorites, and the smell of tomatoes, garlic and basil from the sauce beckoned.

Evan, Holly, and the kids were hunkered down at home. They were planning a movie night camped out in front of the fireplace with blankets, popcorn, and candles nearby in case the power went out. Both houses had generators that would kick in if needed, and I knew, like us, they had lots of board games on hand if they lost power. You learned, living in this province, to always have a backup plan. But the beauty and simplicity of this life was worth some minor inconveniences. I had checked on Dylan and Alex, who assured me they were battened down and ready for when the storm hit their side. Amy's parents were prepared too, although annoyed since they had planned to visit this weekend. I assured them that as soon as the storm finished and the roads were safe, they were welcome. I got on well with my in-laws and enjoyed their company. I knew they were anxious to see us, including the newest member of the family.

I made sure the fire was going, checked dinner preparations, then headed upstairs where my heart wanted to be. As I approached the bedroom, I heard Amy's soft voice talking to Mia.

"Yes, just like that, Sweet Pea. Oh, you are such a quick learner. Now wrap it around her again. Yes, that's right. A perfect swaddle."

"Now I can hold her?"

"Yes."

I stood in the doorway, watching my girls. My beautiful wife, my eldest daughter, and the newest addition, my baby girl, Madison. Or Maddie, as Mia called her.

Mia held her baby sister, cooing down at her. She looked up at Amy. "She's the most beautiful baby ever, Mom."

Amy chuckled, wincing a little as she leaned over, stroking Maddie's cheek. "I think so too."

"I love her so much."

"I know you do."

"I don't care if she's my half sister. She's all ours."

Amy frowned and glanced up, meeting my eyes. I pushed off the doorframe and sauntered in, dropping kisses to all my girls' cheeks. I sat on the ottoman in front of the small love seat where Amy and Mia were, meeting Mia's eyes.

"Who called her your half sister?"

"One of the kids at school."

Amy shook her head. "We're a family. All equal. I love you as much as Maddie, and I didn't give birth to you. Family means love. And we love one another. There are no halves here."

"That's what I told him. I was mad, but I didn't punch him this time."

I met Amy's amused glance. "Oh, this was Oscar again?"

Mia and Oscar were continually on the outs. The day Oscar showed up at school, he had pushed Mia's buttons, and for the first time, I was called to the office, shocked to have been told that my daughter had punched someone. To everyone's shock, Oscar had insisted it was his fault because he teased Mia about her freckles. They had appeared over the summer, a wide band of flecks across the bridge of her nose and onto her cheeks. I thought they made her look even more adorable, but she hated them and he had chosen to tease her about the one thing she was ultrasensitive over. She punched him square in the nose, and Amy and I, along with his parents, were brought in to discuss the matter. The children apologized to each other, shook hands, and swore there would be no more remarks or punching.

Since then, they were alternately friends or enemies. Amy and I thought Oscar harbored a huge crush on Mia and did everything he could to get her attention. I wasn't ready for her to like boys yet, so I was glad when she found him annoying. I dreaded the day he became cute and interesting.

"Good job, Sweet Pea, controlling your temper. I hope you told him off, though."

"I did. He apologized later and told me he thought Maddie was cute. He even texted later to make sure I wasn't still mad."

"He, ah, has your number?" I asked, not sure I was comfortable with the idea.

"We're all part of a group, Dad. I have all their numbers."

"Oh, right. Good." That made me feel better.

"He texts me the most often, though. He says I'm the easiest to talk to."

My relief evaporated, but Amy narrowed her eyes at me and shook her head in a subtle fashion, so I kept my mouth shut. I wasn't sure how I was going to survive the teenage years. Thank God for Amy. She handled the changing hormones and emotions far better than I did. As I discovered, ice cream only soothed some problems.

Mia looked up. "Do you think she'll love me?"

"She already does," Amy assured her. "Look how she cuddles into you. She knows you're her sister."

"Will she mind I'm so much older? Angela and Hannah are so close because they're almost the same age. I'll be gone when she's ten. She won't even know me." Her bottom lip trembled.

"Where are you going?" I asked, trying to tease her out of her sad mood.

She looked at me, rolling her eyes. "I'll be in university, Dad."

I chuckled. "Halifax is an hour away if you go there. Or even if you go elsewhere, you can connect a hundred different ways now. And you being older, you can share your wealth of experience. She'll come to you for advice. If anything, you'll find her annoying. She'll worship you."

"I'll never find her annoying," she replied. "I love her."

I laughed. "I'll remind you of that when she's into your stuff, following you everywhere, and talking your ear off."

Mia smiled, the tears passing. Amy chuckled at my words.

I rubbed her knees. "You okay, Chippy? You look a little pale. Did you overdo it today?"

Maddie's delivery hadn't been easy and had ended with a last-minute cesarean. Amy lost a lot of blood, and I had been frantic thinking I might lose her or the baby. But they had both rebounded, and I was beyond grateful for that. Amy was still recovering, and although she was a rock star, I worried about her overdoing it. Her mom and Holly helped us out the first couple weeks, but Amy insisted she was doing better and had lots of support from Mia and me, so we were finally on our own. Her mom was anxious to return, and the only thing stopping her right now was the blizzard.

"I'm fine."

"How about a nap? The storm is settling in, dinner is ready to pop in the oven, and Mia and I can introduce Maddie to the wonders of board games."

Amy shook her head. "She's three weeks old."

"Perfect age to start. I used to play solitaire with Mia on my shoulder. She rocks that game. Osmosis," I insisted, loving how my teasing made her smile.

I leaned over and took Maddie from Mia. "You go get some games, Sweet Pea. I'll tuck your mom in, and we'll come down."

Mia hurried away. "I'll make some popcorn!"

I peered at the tiny face swaddled in a warm blanket in my arms. Maddie's cheeks were round and soft. Her hair, wisps of golden blonde on her head. When open, her eyes were still blue, soft and wide, just like Amy's. I hoped they stayed that color. She was asleep, one fist having found its way from the blanket and tucked by her face. I bent and kissed her downy cheek. My love for this tiny being shocked me. I would do anything for both of my daughters.

Amy watched us with an indulgent smile.

"She is so perfect," I marveled. "And so tiny. Even smaller than Mia was."

"She'll grow fast. She already has."

"I know." I stared at her in wonder. "Our girl loves to sleep."

"What do you think brought on Mia's worries?" Amy asked.

"Probably seeing Angela and Hannah together yesterday. I noticed she stared at them a lot—the way they laughed and teased. They are very close in age and their relationship. Mia will have a different sort with Maddie, but still amazing, I think. She'll be her mentor and friend."

"I wonder how she'll feel about the age gap between her and the next one," Amy mused.

I gaped at her. "The next one? Amy, you're still recovering. I'm not ready to discuss the next one, or if there'll even be one. Jesus, I'm almost forty-four."

She scoffed. "Whatever. You're the sexiest, youngest forty-four-year-old I know." She regarded me seriously. "If we're going to have another one, it will have to be soon, Simon. It's harder to get pregnant as a woman gets older. It's harder on her too."

"Can we discuss this in a few months? Once you've recovered, I'm allowed to touch you, and we see how this baby affects our life?"

"But you're not saying no?"

I thought about Amy pregnant. Until the last month, it had been a relatively easy one. She had little morning sickness, no problems, and had been happy and content most of the time. Unlike when Kelsey was pregnant with Mia, there were no tantrums, no constant demands, or screaming fits about what the baby was doing to her physically. Amy was thrilled to be pregnant and was as in awe of the changes to her body as I was. I especially enjoyed her second trimester when she couldn't keep her hands off me. Her free spirit and adventuresome nature came out to play fully. I had to admit, I wouldn't mind experiencing that again.

I shook my head to clear it. Sex was off-limits right now, so I couldn't be thinking those thoughts.

"I'm not saying no, Amy. I would never say no to you."

"Okay, then," she agreed easily. "We'll talk later." Then she yawned and rubbed her eyes, suddenly looking exhausted. It happened fast right now.

I lifted Maddie to my shoulder, then stood, helping Amy from the love seat. "To bed with you, Mrs. Fletcher."

"I want to come downstairs and be with you," she argued. "I don't want to be up here alone."

"Then you're on the sofa and napping," I bargained.

"I can do that."

We went down the steps carefully, me holding Maddie with one hand bracing her close, and the other arm wrapped around Amy's waist. She used the handrail for extra support.

"Sheldon called earlier while you were making the lasagna."

"Where is he?"

"Somewhere in the Greek Islands."

"Having a good time?"

"Yes."

"How's Ellie?"

"Married."

I stopped on the stairs and stared at her. "What?"

"They got married yesterday on a beach in Greece."

"Legally?"

"Yep. Witnesses and everything. He said they'd have a party when they got back."

"Holy shit." They had both been adamantly against marriage. Ellie said never again, and Sheldon scoffed, saying a piece of paper made everything change—and not for the better. Apparently, they had both had a change of heart.

"I know. He called and told my parents too. He sounds very happy."

"So, when are they coming home?"

"In a couple of months. He wants to give Ellie a chance to see everything she dreamed of."

"Who knew how far they'd come? How much their life would change when they met each other," I mused. "Funny how you come here for one reason and end up finding your life. Me and you. Evan and Holly. Dylan and Alex. Now your brother and Ellie."

"I know. It's magic."

I grinned and helped her off the last step, noticing another grimace. I guided her to the sofa, and after releasing Maddie to Mia's waiting embrace, I helped Amy lie down, making sure she was comfortable. I bent and kissed her forehead. "It is," I agreed. "Except I think you're the magic one, Chippy. Now sleep, my tired wife. I have our girls, and I'll watch over you."

She smiled, her eyes drifting shut. "You always do."

I stroked a few unruly curls off her face, and she sighed in pleasure, tucking one hand under her cheek. She resembled Maddie so much at the moment, it made my heart ache with tenderness.

This special, wonderful woman who, with her laughter, joy, and light, brought me back to life. Gave me a family. An unexpected chance at happiness. Brought me something I had never experienced before in my adult life. Peace.

My beautiful, free-spirited wife.

I pressed a kiss to her soft lips with a promise.

"And I always will."

Thank you so much for reading AN UNEXPECTED CHANCE. If you are so inclined, reviews are always welcome by me at your retailer.

If you'd like another glimpse into Simon and Amy's

future, click below to grab a little more time with them - Extended Epilogue An Unexpected Chance available at Bookfunnel: https://BookHip.com/ THCSSVS

Did you miss Evan and Holly's story? You can catch up with their HEA by picking up AN UNEXPECTED GIFT.

Enjoy meeting other readers? Lots of fun, with upcoming book talk and giveaways! Check out Melanie Moreland's Minions on Facebook.

Join my newsletter for up-to-date news, sales, book announcements and excerpts (no spam). Click here to sign up Melanie Moreland's newsletter or visit https://bit.ly/MMorelandNewsletter

Visit my website www.melaniemoreland.com

Enjoy reading! Melanie

Titles published under M. Moreland

Insta-Spark Collection

It Started with a Kiss

Christmas Sugar

An Instant Connection

An Unexpected Gift

Harvest of Love

An Unexpected Chance

Following Maggie

Titles published under Melanie Moreland

The Contract Series

The Contract (Contract #1)

The Baby Clause (Contract #2)

The Amendment (Contract #3)

The Addendum (Contract #4)

Vested Interest Series

BAM - The Beginning (Prequel)

Bentley (Vested Interest #1)

Aiden (Vested Interest #2)

Maddox (Vested Interest #3)

Reid (Vested Interest #4)

Van (Vested Interest #5)

Halton (Vested Interest #6)

Sandy (Vested Interest #7)

Vested Interest/ABC Crossover

A Merry Vested Wedding

ABC Corp Series

My Saving Grace (Vested Interest: ABC Corp #1)

Finding Ronan's Heart (Vested Interest: ABC Corp #2)

Loved By Liam (Vested Interest: ABC Corp #3)

Age of Ava (Vested Interest: ABC Corp #4)

Sunshine & Sammy (Vested Interest: ABC Corp #5)

Unscripted With Mila (Vested Interest: ABC Corp #6)

Men of Hidden Justice

The Boss

Second-In-Command

The Commander

The Watcher

The Specialist

Reynolds Restorations

Revved to the Maxx

Breaking The Speed Limit

Shifting Gears

Under The Radar

Full Throttle

Full 360

Mission Cove

The Summer of Us

Standalones

Into the Storm

Beneath the Scars

Over the Fence

The Image of You

Changing Roles

Happily Ever After Collection

Heart Strings

ABOUT M MORELAND

M Moreland is a pen name for NYT/WSJ/USAT international bestselling author Melanie Moreland. She loves writing contemporary romance and needed to find a home for her *bit of naughty along with the nice.*

Insta-Spark collection from M Moreland are complete standalone reads with one thing in common - lots of sweetness and a guaranteed HEA. Instant attraction, little angst - love and happiness abounds.

Melanie lives a happy and content life in a quiet area of Ontario with her beloved husband of thirty-plus years and their rescue cat, Amber. Nothing means more to her than her friends and family, and she cherishes every moment spent with them.

While seriously addicted to coffee, and highly challenged with all things computer-related and technical, she relishes baking, cooking, and trying new recipes for people to sample. She loves to throw dinner parties, and enjoys traveling, here and abroad, but finds coming home is always the best part of any trip.

Melanie loves stories, especially paired with a good wine, and enjoys skydiving (free falling over a fleck of dust) extreme snowboarding (falling down stairs) and piloting her own helicopter (tripping over her own feet.) She's learned happily ever afters, even bumpy ones, are all in how you tell the story.

Melanie is represented by Flavia Viotti at Bookcase Literary Agency. For any questions regarding subsidiary or translation rights please contact her at flavia@bookcaseagency.com

Connect with Melanie

Like reader groups? Lots of fun and giveaways! Check it out Melanie Moreland's Minions

Join my newsletter for up-to-date news, sales, book announcements and excerpts (no spam). Click here to sign up Melanie Moreland's newsletter

or visit https://bit.ly/MMorelandNewsletter

Visit my website www.melaniemoreland.com

facebook.com/authormoreland

twitter.com/morelandmelanie

instagram.com/morelandmelanie

CPSIA information can be obtained
at www.ICGtesting.com
Printed in the USA
LVHW081725190323
741977LV00030BA/464